Maverick in the Sky

D0357676

Maverick in the Sky

**The Aerial Adventures of
World War I Flying Ace Freddie McCall**

Shirlee Smith Matheson

Frontenac House
Calgary, Alberta

Book and cover design: Epix Design
Author photo: Paula Sten
All photographs are from the McCall family; additional scans provided by the
Glenbow Museum of Calgary. The author acknowledges the financial support
of the Alberta Foundation for the Arts.

Library and Archives Canada Cataloguing in Publication
Matheson, Shirlee Smith
        Maverick in the sky : the aerial adventures of World War I flying ace
Freddie McCall / Shirlee Smith Matheson.
Includes bibliographical references and index.
ISBN 978-1-897181-16-4
        1. McCall, Freddie. 2. Fighter pilots--Canada--Biography. 3. World War,
1914-1918--Aerial operations. 4. Stunt flying--Canada--History. 5. Air pilots--
Alberta--Biography. 6. Air pilots--Canada--Biography. I. Title.
TL540.M33M37 2007   629.13092   C2007-906897-9

The publisher acknowledges the support of the Canada Council for the Arts
for our publishing program. We also acknowledge the support of The Alberta
Foundation for the Arts.

Printed and bound in Canada
Published by Frontenac House Ltd.
1138 Frontenac Avenue S.W.
Calgary, Alberta, T2T 1B6, Canada
Tel: 403-245-2491 Fax: 403-245-2380
editor@frontenachouse.com www.frontenachouse.com

This book is dedicated to Fred and Dixie McCall, who so greatly encouraged and assisted me; and to Michale Lang, who asked me: "Why don't you write a book about Freddie?"

Contents

Dogfight

Freddie McCall's military action started as soon as he arrived in France on December 4, 1917, his 22nd birthday. Was he told that the cloth-covered biplane aircraft assigned to him was low and slow? That it was more suited for taking photos of enemy actions or dropping propaganda leaflets than for battle? Whatever the briefing he received before flying over enemy lines, McCall quickly found himself in the thick of aerial combat.

"I was over enemy lines at about 9,000 feet when suddenly two machines of the fastest and best German type came for me. What a glorious battle we had among the clouds, with gunners and infantry watching their respective representatives going for each other!

"The fight lasted about 15 minutes and oh, what a warm time it was! But God seemed to protect me from the 300 bullets the enemy fired, and after I put about 150 at once into his aircraft, his engine stopped and down he went. He waved goodbye as he went down and I waved back at him, so I suppose there were no hard feelings ...

"I saw him crash into the wire in front of the trenches. He may not have been killed but his machine was in an awful mess after striking the ground. When the other Hun saw his pal go down, he didn't take long to clear off the horizon, I can tell you. When I landed I found I had six holes in my machine and my wireless had been cut off."

And so began the flying career of the fearless Freddie McCall. His amazing daring, ability, and luck would be put to the test again and again.

CHAPTER 1

The Great War

ON SEPTEMBER 26, 1916, SERGEANT FREDDIE MCCALL FOUND HIMSELF ON AN OVERSEAS VOYAGE WITH NO GUARANTEE OF A RETURN TRIP HOME. SEVEN SHORT MONTHS EARLIER, HE HAD SIGNED UP AT THE CALGARY RECRUITMENT OFFICE TO FIGHT FOR HIS COUNTRY AND HIS SCOTTISH FOREBEARS. IT WAS AN HONOURABLE THING TO DO, AND 21-YEAR-OLD FREDDIE CAME FROM AN HONOURABLE FAMILY.

Freddie's father, James, was chief engineer at Calgary's electric plant, a Rotarian, and a charter member of the Grand Lodge of Alberta, Ancient Free and Accepted Masons. His community work included erecting a monument in Central Park in 1914 to honour veterans of the South African War. The McCall family (James and his wife, Agnes, with daughters Christine and Marjorie and son Freddie) lived comfortably in their two-storey home on 13 Avenue South West, and attended the Grace Presbyterian Church nearby.

Acquaintances and colleagues of the time recall young Freddie as being friendly and popular, as well as active in sporting events and his cadet corps. After completing his high school education, he'd gone to work at the city's Lights Department as a "trouble man", sent out on call to fix electrical problems. He'd been there three years when rumours of war began to circulate. Like many other Canadian boys of his day, he was ready for some action.

McCall was accepted for service in the 175th Overseas Battalion, Alberta Regiment of the Canadian Expeditionary Force. Immediately following his medical exam, which recorded him as 5' 6" tall and weighing 140 pounds, with brown eyes, auburn hair, and a fair complexion, his basic training started at Sarcee Military Camp in Calgary.

INITIAL TRAINING

McCall's diary entry on September 4, 1916, outlined the qualifications of an instructor: "Know the subject thoroughly, be patient, and be able to detect and remedy faults." Then he'd added, "Words of command are seldom required. One must lead by example rather than word of mouth." He would learn and apply this lesson particularly well. On completion of Infantry School, Private McCall was promoted to sergeant and sent off to England with his unit.

Private Freddie McCall poses in his Army uniform just after volunteering to serve in The Great War.

England proved to be no fun. Wallowing in ankle-deep mud on Salisbury Plain, McCall could only watch as the British fliers zoomed in from the Front. On February 23, the first night-bomber squadron of the war set off for France to bomb German installations. Fighting the "Huns", as they called the Germans (after Attila's fierce tribe that had invaded the Roman Empire in the fifth century), would surely be better from an aircraft than across muddy trenches. Despite his miserable, muddy existence, McCall continued to excel and he received a promotion to lieutenant.

At this point he decided that he wanted to become a flier. He applied to join the Royal Flying Corps (RFC), which was the only route then available for Canadians serving overseas who

Maverick in the Sky

Sergeant Freddie McCall with family prior to going overseas. L to R: Freddie, his mother Agnes, brother-in-law Percy Thompson, sister Christine Thompson, sister Marjorie McCall. Front row: nephew Art Thompson and Freddie's father James McCall (kneeling).

wanted to fly, and on March 1, 1917, he reported to the School of Aeronautics at Reading in Berkshire for ground school. Although sick with the flu and suffering intensely from the cold, windy weather, he quickly forgot his physical discomforts as he listened, entranced, to the wondrous, and often frightening, heroic stories of the early British pilots and their planes.

THE RFC

The Royal Flying Corps had been formed in 1912 as the overland air arm of the British military, with the motto *Per Ardua ad Astra* — "Through Adversity to the Stars". McCall was about to discover for himself that the word "adversity" was indeed appropriate. The RFC had started out tough and became progressively tougher. The corps experienced its first crash, over Salisbury Plain, only six weeks after its formation and both the captain and observer had been killed. The formal response to the accident? "Flying will continue this evening as usual."

As McCall found out then and later commented, "When war broke out in 1914, little had been done in perfecting aircraft for war purposes. The machines that went to France in the early stages were very slow and clumsy. They could not climb to any height worth mentioning, and were equipped with no armaments whatsoever." During the first months of combat flying, pilots on both sides were armed with only pistols and rifles! Allied pilots were even sent without parachutes, as it was considered a sign of weakness to anticipate the need to bail out.

While a pilot struggled to keep his rickety little aircraft aloft *and* shoot at the enemy, he'd also had to tap out reconnaissance information via a wireless telegraph and transmit it to the ground forces. There were no airfields at the beginning of the war, and so the squadrons had to land on the handiest grassy field. Ground support, consisting of mechanics, fuelling systems, and portable hangars, kitchens, and accommodation, followed later.

Amidst these difficult and primitive conditions, the officers in the Flying Corps were charged with keeping their men active. If an airman had survived a near-miss or a crash, or if one of the squadron's aircraft failed to return, the survivors would be quickly sent back into the air. Airmen learned not to stare long at the empty chair at the mess table or the unoccupied bunk nearby, and to lustily sing along with the rest of the boys:

> *So… stand by your glasses steady,*
> *This world is a world of lies,*
> *Here's a toast to the dead already;*
> *Hurrah for the next man who dies!*

DOGFIGHTS AND FLYING CIRCUSES

Fortunately for McCall, by 1917 aircraft capabilities had come a long way. Small pursuit aircraft were achieving speeds of 150 mph, and reaching altitudes of 24,000 feet; slower bombers could carry two tons of bombs. Thus equipped, the Flying Corps was sent out to observe enemy locations and movements, to adjust artillery fire on to designated targets, photograph enemy locations, and bomb enemy strongholds. They also engaged enemy aircraft in aerial combat, aptly known as "dogfights." Fliers would circle one another and manoeuvre their aircraft until one had the advantage and could close in for the kill. In the conflict that had already been going on for three gruelling years, both sides were constantly producing more modern machinery while expediting the training of flight crews.

Germany had developed a seemingly unbeatable aerial arrangement called a Flying Circus: an armada of 40 to 50 aircraft that roamed sectors along the front lines in search of the enemy. The Allies formed their squadrons into similar fearsome groups that swept across German lines. Just one month after McCall had begun his theory and ground school and in the first week of "Bloody April" 1917, the RFC lost 75 aircraft in action. By the end of the month, the fatality score stood at 150 aircraft and 316 aircrew. Manfred von Richthofen (The Red Baron), Germany's most noted and feared fighter pilot, was responsible for downing 22 of those aircraft that month.

IN THE AIR AT LAST

Notwithstanding the odds, McCall was itching to get into the action as he continued his flight instruction with some airtime. "June 17, 1917: Went up for the first time with Capt. Lloyd in Maurice Farman Shorthorn [aircraft] at 6:30 p.m."

His next flight was more exciting: "Up in the DH6 with Capt. Lloyd on formation flight to York where we stunted — Immelmann Turns — 2,300 feet for 110 minutes." McCall was eager to emulate the skills of other Allied, as well as enemy, pilots. Max Immelmann, a German flying ace, was famous for inverting his aircraft at the top of a loop to roll it back to an upright position, but at a higher altitude and with an instant heading change of 180 degrees. But even the best fliers were subject to fate, and McCall was aware that Immelmann himself had met his death just the year before, after scoring 17 aerial victories. McCall concentrated on perfecting the Immelmann Turns, in case the tricky manoeuvre could save his life some day.

Around the aerodrome, while his fellow British squadron officers were flying captured enemy aircraft, stripped of their German markings, for practice and knowledge of the enemy's capabilities, McCall and his classmates were taught to detect the deadly gas attacks perpetrated by their enemy. They had to be ready for anything. McCall was rapidly familiarizing himself with the Curtiss trainer, Bristol scout, and BE-2E and RE-8 observation biplanes when, in June 1917, German bombers attacked London with incredible and unmatched fury. The RFC seemed helpless to stop them.

Combat aircraft, and those who flew and fixed them, were making the newspaper headlines, showing that aviation was not only for romantic dreamers. That fall of 1917, 11 Zeppelin airships bombed Britain in a deadly silent raid. In November, just after McCall was posted to No. 17 Training Squadron in Yatesbury, RFC aircraft dropped bombs on anti-tank guns to clear a path for Allied armies to advance in the Battle of Cambrai.

Aviation was being touted as the way to win the war, and Lieut. Freddie McCall would soon be at its forefront, battling expert enemy fighter pilots such as the Red Baron. He received his wings at Tadcaster on November 22, 1917, then attended Artillery and Infantry Cooperation School in Hurley Park for final training as an air observer pilot. Trained very quickly and effectively, McCall was now considered prepared and more than ready for battle. He'd had exactly one hour and 40 minutes of actual experience in the air.

CHAPTER 2

Combat Action

LIEUT. McCALL'S FIRST POSTING AS A FULL-FLEDGED PILOT
WAS TO FLY ARTILLERY OBSERVATION AND BOMBING MISSIONS
WITH No. 13 RFC SQUADRON. WOULD No. 13 PROVE TO BE
A LUCKY OR UNLUCKY NUMBER FOR McCALL? AVIATORS
HAD TO CONVINCE THEMSELVES THEY WERE INVULNERABLE.
"THOSE OTHERS, WELL, THEY MADE A MISTAKE. I WON'T."

THE LOW, SLOW AIRCRAFT

McCall was assigned to fly the slow open-cockpit two-seater
RE-8 (Reconnaissance Experimental) observation aircraft,
nicknamed the "Harry Tate" after a music-hall comedian. The
RE-8 was said to be the clumsiest plane in Allied service, and
considered "cold meat" for German aviators. McCall was well
aware that an entire patrol of RE-8s had met the Red Baron's
Flying Circus earlier that year. None of the six Allied aircraft
had returned from the enemy lines, and only two crew members had survived.

Initially meant for scouting, the aircraft became more
formidable once firearms were added. By the time McCall
was assigned to fly the RE-8 in early December of 1917, the
aircraft's climb and speed capabilities had also improved. The
RE-8 was not easily manoeuvred, however, and its small fin
and rudder hampered directional stability, resulting in a number of fatal stall-spin crashes.

From dawn to dusk, weather permitting, squadrons of
this heavily armed but awkward aircraft took turns patrolling
along the battle front. Their main focus was to support their
ground forces' artillery, and to seek out the enemy forces and
report their locations and activities. McCall set his mind to

putting theory into practice. He knew his life would depend on smart manoeuvres.

On January 6, 1918, Lieut. McCall and 2nd Lieut. Farrington were assigned a reconnaissance patrol far over the enemy line. Their mission was to gather intelligence, but they always had to expect sudden engagement with enemy fighter aircraft. Fortunately, the machine gun on their RE-8 was synchronized with the propeller to fire between its moving blades. "This innovation was crucial to combat aircraft," McCall later wrote. "To have a gun mounted in the 'V' of the engine was ideal; it was directly in front of the pilot's eye, easy to maintain when in flight, and the oil would be kept warm in cold altitudes." The second armament was a Lewis machine gun, mainly for operation by the observer.

Lieutenant McCall studies aerial photos before leaving on a winter reconnaissance mission.

In aerial combat, the main objective was to bring the enemy pilot and his fuel tank, engine, and principal controls into a direct line of fire. A burst of tracer bullets striking the fuel tank above the level of the fuel would usually set the aircraft

Maverick in the Sky

on fire. But if the enemy suddenly turned and came toward him, the pilot had to cease firing, and scram upward to escape the line of fire. If possible, he should move to another position of advantage, and fire again.

McCall and Farrington had been trained that the advantage in aerial combat was usually height. When and if their more experienced leader on the patrol spotted enemy aircraft, he would try to warn his followers by a pre-arranged signal such as firing a red light from his Very [signal] pistol or dipping his wings, so they could evade potential trouble.

Equipped with these minimal instructions, the novice Lieut. McCall took off from the aerodrome and resolutely piloted the RE-8 over the enemy lines. The patrol soared as high as 15,000 feet over the front line. Observer Farrington was busy taking photographs over Estaires when, without warning, they came under attack by two German Albatros scouts. These streamlined single-scat biplanes, armed with two machine guns, had contributed greatly to Germany's domination of the Western Front throughout the first half of 1917.

McCall knew the clumsy old RE-8 was no match for the fast, agile Albatros. He started for home, but realized there was no time to make it to safety. The Germans overtook the slower RE-8 and attacked from side to side, top to bottom, and up from the rear, avoiding frontal attack whenever possible, firing hundreds of rounds. McCall and Farrington fired back as McCall put the aircraft through every imaginable move to keep out of range. For 15 long minutes he dived, soared, and swerved.

And then, McCall saw an opportunity for attack: one Albatros was flying below him. He dove on it, as fire blazed from both his and Farrington's guns. As McCall manoeuvred the RE-8 close to the Albatros, Farrington seized an opportunity to fire into its engine. The Albatros dropped into a steep glide, its propeller stilled. They saw it spiral down over No Man's Land, the area between the trenches of the opposing forces. The second enemy aircraft fled.

Combat Action

McCall and Farrington flew home, their adrenalin pumping, their RE-8 riddled with bullet holes, and their wireless apparatus damaged and useless. Victory #1 (shared with Farrington) was confirmed later, to set up what would soon become McCall's amazing scoreboard.

CONSPICUOUS GALLANTRY

Lieut. McCall went into the air nearly every day that was flyable. In his reconnaissance reports, he continued to observe the constant movements and flashes of enemy guns, bombs, and explosions, and take photographs back to headquarters. He also carried out artillery patrols, which meant supporting an artillery battery by providing an air observation post from his aircraft. Informed of the target and with an overall view of the enemy location, he could observe the fall of friendly artillery and help them to zero in on the target.

As McCall gained airtime, he also became offensively bolder. Sighting a German aircraft at a higher altitude, the patrol would try to reach its level before attacking. When this wasn't possible, the leader — often McCall, as he became more experienced — held his patrol together, "permitting" the enemy flier to commence his dive. As the enemy came within firing range, the patrol would make an "about turn" to come underneath and quickly fire off some rounds. The enemy was forced to pull out of his dive, and the move was repeated until all the machines were on the same level. As many as 70 aircraft might join in a single aerial dogfight. The battles were fast and furious, and, as McCall would say, "Grim fate attended to the rest."

The continued excellence of his artillery patrols brought him his first decoration, the Military Cross (MC), for "conspicuous gallantry and devotion to duty; a fine example of courage and determination on all occasions."

On March 6, McCall and Farrington were together again on photographic patrol in an RE-8, and, despite poor visibility, had climbed to 10,000 feet. Out of the gloom, a dark ghost zoomed straight toward them. Its black paint, with markings of black crosses inside white circles, identified it as an Albatros. McCall turned to face his attacker and dived on the Albatros, firing as he did so. The burst of machine-gun fire from the RE-8 took the enemy pilot by surprise. He turned his aircraft, intending to come under the RE-8, which gave Farrington his chance to fire from his Lewis gun. The Albatros fell from the sky, smoke pluming from its engine. It was a hit, but to be sure, McCall followed him down, continuing to fire the forward Vickers gun. From 4,000 feet over the Sensee River, he watched the Albatros crash — his second recorded victory. When McCall saw two enemy aircraft swooping in to avenge their lost brother, he quickly exited. He knew to pick his battles.

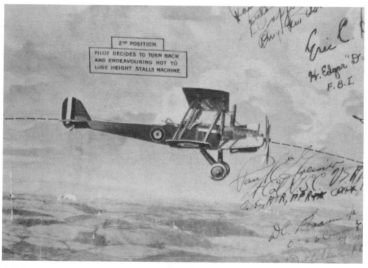

A British RE-8 reconnaissance airplane was McCall's first combat machine.

On March 21, 1918, No. 13 Squadron was sent flying south over enemy lines. Although reconnaissance was still their primary role, they were told to throw everything they had into the battle, to help attack German troops on the ground. Their RE-8s carried bomb loads as well as their full capacity of rounds and belts of ammunition. The element of surprise would be paramount for McCall and his patrollers. The fighting was ferocious, and by nightfall, 17 RFC squadrons had to evacuate their airfields to avoid being overtaken and occupied by attacking enemy ground forces.

On March 28, McCall recorded his third victory while on artillery patrol over Allied lines at 3,000 feet. He observed two Rumpler two-seaters cross the lines very low and later reported, "I dived on the rear machine and fired 200 rounds at 100 yards range. The observer ceased firing at me and collapsed in the fuselage. Machine crashed in enemy's lines." With the observer dead in one aircraft and his pilot either wounded or killed, the severely damaged aircraft plunged to its fate over Estaires. The second Rumpler headed for home to avoid the fate of his comrade.

McCall was still in the initial stages of his military flying, but his agility was bringing astounding results, especially considering how slow and clumsy the RE-8 was. Even so, during March 1918, the Germans gained air superiority over the river Somme (in the second notable battle at that location), with some 730 aircraft, including 326 fighters, on the Western Front. The RFC had only 579 aircraft, of which 261 were fighters. The RFC and Royal Naval Air Service (RNAS) squadrons' low-level attacks were having some effect, however, in their roles of reconnaissance, adjustment of artillery fire, and bombing attacks on the enemy's strongholds. Their efforts marked the first time in history that the large-scale use of air power had a direct influence on the successful outcome of a land battle.

Number 13 had proved lucky for McCall, at least so far. After flying a total of 123 hours and 20 minutes with No. 13 Squadron, he had tallied five victories, which qualified him as an allied ace. Lieut. McCall was given a well-earned two-week leave and on April 25, 1918, he appeared before His Majesty King George V at Buckingham Palace to have the Military Cross pinned to his tunic.

Meanwhile, the war was becoming increasingly violent, with fighting on multiple fronts involving more countries. When the United States of America entered the conflict it was urged to send extra troops to Europe, even if they were untrained. The Allied situation was grave. Was Germany unbeatable? At one time during those desperate days in April 1918, Field Marshal Sir Douglas Haig, the British Commander-in-Chief, acknowledged, "Our backs are to the wall," and forbade further retreat.

Then, while McCall was still in London, Germany's Red Baron was killed in action. He'd risked flying his red Fokker DR.I on an uncommonly long and low-level flight behind the Australian front in avid pursuit of Canadian fighter pilot Wop May. The elite squadron of pilots under von Richthofen's command refused to believe his death until the British dropped a message canister over Germany with a photograph of the corpse to confirm it. The British buried the well-respected Red Baron with full military honours; his 80 victories had distinguished him as the top-scoring pilot in the war. But other pilots knew that the Red Baron had made a colossal mistake, an error against his training. If he could fall, others could also be subject to such lapses of judgement. His death sent a message that even the mightiest warriors were subject to "grim fate".

CHAPTER 3

Aerial Adventures

IN THE SPRING OF 1918, THE RFC WAS RENAMED THE ROYAL AIR FORCE (RAF) AND BECAME THE FIRST AIR FORCE TO BE INDEPENDENT OF EITHER THE NAVY OR ARMY. APART FROM THE NEW CAP BADGE AND WING INSIGNIA DESIGN, LIEUT. MCCALL WOULDN'T HAVE NOTICED ANY CHANGES.

In May 1918, McCall was transferred from his reconnaissance role to an active fighter squadron and posted to No. 41 Squadron. He was excited to be recognized as fighter pilot material, and to learn that he'd be flying the Royal Aircraft Factory Scout Experimental SE-5a, a single-seat aircraft that had gone into action just the year before. This little biplane was powered by a 200-hp Wolseley Viper V8 engine that sent it climbing like a rocket to 23,000 feet. Its top speed was 132 mph at an altitude of 6,500 feet, making it the fastest single-seat fighter at the Front. Constructed of wood and fabric, it was light, extremely manoeuvrable, and easy to control.

Most of the top RAF aces flew the SE-5a fighter, and McCall was now recognized as being part of this elite group. Only the Sopwith Camel — less forgiving and more difficult to fly — would destroy more enemy aircraft. Like the RE-8, the SE-5a was heavily armed. A Vickers machine gun, synchronized to fire through the propeller blades, was mounted on the top left side of the fuselage. A Lewis gun, located above the centre section on the upper wing, could be fired by pulling the trigger, or by a cable that ran from the trigger to the cockpit with an end ring. The barrel could also be pointed upward so the pilot could fire at enemy aircraft flying above him — a distinct advantage enabling the pilot to position himself directly below and out of the enemy's sight.

Maverick in the Sky

Especially valuable was that the Lewis could be pulled back down into the cockpit for unloading and reloading the ammunition drums, and for clearing stoppages if it jammed (which was often). But McCall came to realize that this operation was not easy. He'd have to change position in his seat, and perhaps unbuckle his safety harness. Both hands might be required to pull the gun down the curved rail (called the Foster mount) to remove the spent ammunition drum and replace it with a new one. In this aircraft, McCall had no observer to help him — he was on his own.

And finally, in addition to the Vickers and Lewis guns, the SE-5a had a mechanism for carrying bombs under the fuselage.

On May 19 and 20, 1918, the German air force dispatched 43 bombers in its most severe air attack to date on Britain. The air battle was heating up, but in the SE-5a, McCall was prepared for the challenge. If he spotted the enemy at a lower altitude, he knew to manoeuvre his aircraft to a position of attack down the sun's rays, or out from cloud concealment. Then he would dive as fast as possible while taking care that no enemy fliers hovered above to trap him. He also had to keep away from the front of enemy aircraft, with their guns pointing straight ahead. Once he'd slipped under an enemy's tail plane, McCall would match its speed, take careful aim through the telescopic sight, and fire into the target aircraft by pressing trigger levers on the control stick.

A week or so later, observing a two-seater biplane flying at 3,000 feet, he dived on it out of the sun. The enemy pilot spotted him and quickly turned south while firing back from a 1,000-yard range, hitting a longeron (main support spar) in the fuselage. The DFW (Deutsche Flugzeug-Werke) then dove off to the east. McCall followed, executing a left-hand, half-roll dive at 200 mph to get below the enemy aircraft. From 50 feet behind, he could see the observer turned in his swivel chair to face his pilot, likely discussing their strike and not noticing McCall coming up from behind. McCall pressed two levers on the control stick that operated both machine guns. Nothing! Due to lack of pressure in the oil gear system, the Vickers gun failed to fire, but then McCall heard four distinct rounds leaving the Lewis gun.

At the burst of sound, the enemy observer swivelled in his chair and grabbed for his gun. Too late. McCall's fire from beneath had caught their fuel tank bang-on. Smoke billowed from the enemy aircraft, followed by a burst of flame that engulfed all but its nose. Burning like a torch, the DFW dropped, spiralling out of control. McCall glanced back to see the panic-stricken observer dive from his flaming plane and fall thousands of feet to the ground. The pilot, strapped in, was forced to go down with his aircraft.

COLLEAGUES AT WAR

This was war, and McCall had to remind himself that each man was following his training. Firmly at the controls of the tough and agile SE-5a biplane, McCall did not let up. Nor did his pal — another ace in the making — Captain William Gordon Claxton. A fellow prairie boy in No. 41 Squadron, he was nicknamed "Dozy" because of his refusal to get excited no matter how dangerous the action might become. Freddie and Dozy formed a lasting friendship and, while in the air over the Western Front piloting SE-5as, became a formidable air combat team.

On June 12, 1918, while flying over Compiègne at 13,000 feet, McCall's leader spotted eight Albatros scouts below. He signalled to the SE-5a formation to dive on the patrol from the sun. Getting on the tail of one straggler, McCall shot off a burst of fire. He watched his target — and what would make Victory #10 — fall 2,000 feet. Then he found himself under attack from behind. An Immelmann Turn brought his aircraft around and onto the tail of his attacker. The enemy aircraft dropped away. McCall followed, shooting a number of bursts at close range. He left this Albatros after watching it land in a field and stop suddenly, remaining upright.

Maverick in the Sky

Freddie relaxing in his quarters in France.

Meanwhile, Claxton came down on the tail of another enemy aircraft, which also landed in a field. Although these aircraft were driven down by McCall and Claxton, their squadron commander decided they could not be claimed because they had remained upright after landing.

An hour later, over La Motte, McCall spotted an enemy DFW two-seater aircraft flying north at 3,000 feet. He followed it overtop of the clouds as the enemy passed beneath, and then dived when he saw it emerge into clear air. When he was within 75 yards of its tail, McCall opened fire, and continued until he had used up 600 rounds of ammunition. The practice, he'd always been told tongue-in-cheek, was to not bring ammo home, but to "leave it with the Germans." He climbed up and circled above to watch the enemy aircraft fall in a steep dive.

After another successful kill the next day, McCall broke away to clear a stoppage in his Vickers gun, just in time to see

Claxton flying west at very low altitude under heavy attack by anti-aircraft fire. He followed Claxton to see him land safely behind French lines, and then returned for more action.

Since April 1918, the German air force had been flying the deadly Fokker D.VIIs. The Red Baron's Flying Circus, made up of Germany's finest fighter pilots, was thus equipped. The sturdy single-seat fighter biplane was fast, and could out-manoeuvre most of the Allied aircraft of the time. But on June 16, McCall's patrol ran into a flight of 10 German Fokker tri-planes and biplanes. McCall dived on one and got in a burst at close range. The Fokker D.VII went down and was confirmed destroyed southwest of Combles (Victory #13). Although the remainder of the German formation made a valiant attempt to shoot up McCall's SE-5a, he managed to make it safely back to his aerodrome.

ALL IN A DAY'S WORK

For his further victories, Lieut. McCall was awarded the Bar to the Military Cross (signifying that the Military Cross was awarded twice). He would later comment modestly, "The first

Captain McCall, DSO, MC & Bar, DFC, with fellow aviator (identity unknown).

Maverick in the Sky

15 aircraft I brought down were captured in as many differ-ent ways, but after that I became accustomed to the differ-ent methods of attack and defence, and found it more in the nature of a risky day's work rather than each engagement a hazardous adventure."

McCall was out again on June 28, over enemy lines at 18,000 feet, leading a scouting patrol of five aircraft, when he encountered a patrol of 11 Albatros scouts flying south, paral-lel to the front lines. His formation manoeuvred above and to the rear of the enemy patrol, to dive on the German leader in a surprise attack. An Albatros scout, a Pfalz, and a Halberstadt went down over Bray.

When McCall heard a burst of machine gun fire from above, a quick half-roll followed by a steep right-hand climb-ing turn brought him out of range of the Albatros guns. The German formation broke up and dove to the east, just as a sec ond patrol of seven enemy scouts emerged. This attack, and the British counter-attack, gave McCall his fourth victory of the day and a total score of 19.

Two days later, on June 30, Lieut. McCall was promoted to captain. That day, after four further kills, he returned to the aerodrome to refuel and replenish his ammunition. Charged with energy, he went into the air once more and at 5:45 p.m. sent an Albatros D.V out of control east of Albert (Victory #24). He discovered that his buddy Claxton had also made five kills that same day, both of them matching the Canadian record of Colonel Billy Bishop.

McCall's reputation as a sharp-shooting pilot was as-sured with 16 victories during the month of June alone. In July, he brought down seven more enemy aircraft, the last two shared with his friend Claxton. In August, McCall was awarded the Distinguished Flying Cross (DFC). "His determination and tenacity in attack is remarkable," read the citation. "On one occasion, whilst acting as escort to reconnaissance machines, he shot down an enemy machine which attempted to interrupt their work; he was then attacked by three enemy scouts which, however, he skilfully managed to elude."

McCall was also honoured with the Distinguished Service Order (DSO) — the ultimate thanks from the leader of a nation under siege. This citation named McCall "a brilliant and gallant officer ... His courage and offensive spirit has inspired all who serve with him."

TROUBLE MAN

McCall had certainly done his part in the war — but would he suffer later? Sometimes airmen broke down when a particular kill got to them — the unforgettable sight of an enemy pilot's horror, or the accusing flash of their eyes, from an aircraft engulfed in flames and corkscrewing in its death spiral. McCall had heard more than one victorious pilot suddenly wake up screaming in his bunk. He knew the only way to survive mentally was to keep his emotions under control.

Physical survival was another thing. Most successful pilots suffered from altitude sickness from flying at altitudes over 10,000 feet without oxygen. At these heights they also suffered from severe cold and wind blasts, even though they wore wool-lined leather flying suits, boots, helmets, and heavy gauntlets on their hands. Their silk scarves prevented neck abrasions as they continuously looked about for enemy aircraft, and goggles protected their eyes from wind and oil spatters. The aircraft engines were lubricated by castor oil, which would come back as a mist into the pilot's face and inevitably would be inhaled into the lungs. These were the hazards — if one survived enemy fire!

McCall was also disturbed by the images of what the foot soldiers were enduring in those cold, miserable, vermin-infested and mud-flooded trenches. And the horses were no less affected. McCall had seen them wallowing up to their stomachs in mud as they strained to pull armaments through the rain-soaked battlefields of France. What would happen to them if they survived the war? Would they return as heroes, too? Even though he was flying above these scenes, McCall could not help but be affected by what he saw going on below. No wonder he was motivated to do his best.

August 1918 got off to a quick start when McCall sent an Albatros two-seater out of control over Cantalmaison on August 1, giving him Victory #32. On August 4, he netted two observation balloons between Caix and Quesnel, counted apart from the downed aircraft. On August 9, No. 41 Squadron brought down nine enemy aircraft. During his own dogfight, two of McCall's engine cylinders were blown off. Still, he managed to land the heavily damaged SE-5a three miles behind French lines at Beiny. That same day his friend Lieut. Claxton destroyed a balloon near Bray and in the afternoon shot down two Fokker biplanes. Afterward, McCall calmly discussed the day with Claxton, just as he would have done with a co worker at home, when he was a "trouble man" at the electric plant. McCall had become a "trouble man" in the war, too.

The men avoided thinking of home too much. They couldn't afford to become sentimental over thoughts about their wives and kids or parents, or sisters and brothers, or even the family dog. But it was nice to receive letters and packages of socks and candy, to know the folks were rooting for them, appreciative of their efforts, and awaiting their safe return.

Although the RAF claimed 177 enemy kills during the week of August 5–11, 1918, they were not easy victories. The air force lost 150 — nearly 25 percent — of its aircraft. That month the RAF made intensive fighter sweeps across the Western Front, with Sopwith Camels flying at 10,000 feet, SE-5s at 14,000 feet, and Bristol Fighters at 18,000 feet.

Friendly Enemy

No. 41 Squadron was in the midst of it all. McCall's 36th victory on August 11 was quite strange. At 9:15 a.m. he encountered seven Fokker D.VII biplanes flying east, north of Bayonvillers. He dived on one and fired a short burst at close range, and then suddenly saw the top half of the enemy aircraft's rudder fly off and sail past his own aircraft. Obviously unable to steer, the German pilot was forced down inside Allied lines. McCall continued to chase three other Fokkers, and by 9:25 a.m. he had scored his 37th victory and what would be his last officially recorded strike.

When he came in later that day to record these incidents, he discovered that the pilot of the Fokker forced down behind British lines was alive and had been taken captive. For some reason McCall said he felt compelled "to rescue the German pilot from overzealous Tommies" (the name commonly given to British soldiers after the poem "Tommy" by Rudyard Kipling).

McCall escorted the pilot, whose name he learned was Fritz Blumenthal, to squadron headquarters to await the arrival of the prisoner of war escort. Having attended a British school before the war, Blumenthal spoke English. When he told McCall he was supposed to be married the following day, McCall decided that the bride-to-be should at least be notified that her groom was alive. The next day he flew over Blumenthal's German aerodrome and dropped a canister containing a message that the wedding would have to be delayed. After the war, Blumenthal wrote to thank McCall for this exceptional courtesy — and to report that he had been belatedly, but happily, married. He even sent along a piece of his Iron Cross ribbon. The two "enemies" continued to correspond — proving that even in the bitterest fighting fields there could be compassion.

LAST CALL

August 17 saw McCall's last, incredible, battle. The formation was on patrol far over the German lines at 15,000 feet when they were attacked by an enemy squadron. During fierce fighting over Ypres, McCall and Claxton became separated from the rest of their patrol. Wingtip to wingtip, they fought off their aggressors. Then the first German squadron was joined by a second to bring the attacking Flying Circus aircraft to 40 against two. The two squadron mates, caught in a funnel of fire from the sweeping dives of the German aircraft, fought back vigorously. Both pilots fired round after round while attempting to head back toward British lines, and were getting close to home when Claxton's aircraft took a hit. McCall caught sight of it spiralling down, out of control and disappearing behind German lines. There was nothing he could do but try to get himself out of there. He finally made it safely to his home aerodrome.

Although it has been reported that McCall and Claxton each brought down three enemy aircraft during this amazing dogfight, no victories were officially recorded for either airman on this date. McCall later discovered that Claxton had been pulled from his wrecked aircraft and taken to the hospital. There, a German surgeon had skilfully operated on his fractured skull, and saved his life. Claxton spent the rest of the war as a prisoner.

All this may have been finally too much for McCall. With Blumenthal, he'd seen the face of his enemy, up close, perhaps too close. Now his friend Claxton was out of commission, lucky to be alive. On August 19, 1918, McCall fell ill. A deadly influenza epidemic was raging throughout the world, killing people off in parallel to the war effort. It would be a bitter irony if McCall had survived aerial combat only to be knocked out by a flu bug. He was taken to a hospital in England, and from there transferred to Canada on a recommended three-month "home service" leave.

McCall's records during his posting with No. 41 Squadron documented 100 missions, equalling 156 hours 30 minutes in the air, in the SE-5a. He had flown a total of 279.50 combat hours and was officially credited with downing 37 enemy aircraft. He reportedly held the record for the "highest six day bag" ever recorded by a Great War pilot: 14 confirmed kills. For all of his efforts, McCall had already been awarded four major decorations and could wear the British War Medal with an oak leaf. He would also receive a Victory Medal, to be presented following the cessation of the war. In his Official Record, only one word appears under the heading of Adverse Reports: Nil.

CHAPTER 4

Canada: Home of the Brave

EVERYONE WAS TRYING TO SHAKE MCCALL'S HAND OR TOUCH HIS UNIFORM, WHICH WAS EMBLAZONED IMPRESSIVELY WITH ALL HIS MEDALS AND RIBBONS. "YES, I'M HOME FOR A SHORT LEAVE," HE EXPLAINED TO HIS GREETERS. "I'LL BE GOING BACK." FOLLOWING CONVALESCENCE IN ENGLAND, CAPTAIN MCCALL HAD ARRIVED HOME AS CANADA'S FIFTH-RANKING AIR ACE IN THE WAR. "ROYAL WELCOME TO FRED MCCALL, CALGARY FIGHTER" READ THE HEADLINES OF HIS HOME-TOWN NEWSPAPER. MEMBERS OF THE BOYS' NAVAL BRIGADE GREETED HIM AT CALGARY'S CPR STATION, AND THE VETERANS' BAND PLAYED "SEE, THE CONQUERING HERO COMES!" TO RESOUNDING APPLAUSE.

The gathered multitude, which included Freddie's parents and sisters, had rushed the train. They didn't just stand back to let the decorated hero alight in a dignified manner. McCall was hauled through the train window and tossed into the arms of Jack Miller, the city clerk, and his old boss, R.A. Brown, the city electrician, to be ceremoniously carried through the crowd to a car draped in the flags of the Allied countries.

Looking smashing in his air force blues and colourful medals, McCall found himself invited to give dinner speeches everywhere from his local Masonic lodge to the Rotary club, and to lend his presence to the sale of war bonds to help pay for Canada's contribution to the war effort. "What was it was like over there?" people demanded of the real live war hero. He tried not to disappoint his audiences. McCall was a good storyteller, with a vivid recall for details — just what the people at home wanted. He could be comical while retaining the serious and reflective countenance of a man who'd witnessed incredible sights.

WAR STORIES

"One fine day in May in the fourth year of the world war, I left my aerodrome some five or six miles behind our front lines to do a two-hour patrol over the German lines in search of enemy aircraft . . ." McCall began at a war bonds fundraising event. "Seated in my tiny but powerful scout and armed with two rapid-fire guns, I quickly rose from the ground and climbed toward the German lines, arriving there in about 10 minutes at a height of 10,000 feet. Finding an aircraft in enemy territory, viewing its markings to identify it as the enemy, and noting it was not being shot at by the Allies' anti-aircraft, I decided to dive in on it.

"Rolling over on one side, I dropped behind him at a speed of 180 mph. When I was some distance behind him and slightly below his level, I zoomed out of my dive toward the tail of the machine. Throttling my machine to the speed of his, I found that I was in an ideal position to attack, being 25 feet to the rear of, and four feet below, his tail plane, which protected me from the observer's gun."

He leaned forward over the podium, and paused before detailing the action — the part of the story the audience was waiting, yet dreading, to hear.

"The observer in this two-seater wheeled about, but he couldn't fire at me without the danger of damaging his own machine. However, before I could draw a bead on him, the pilot rose to the occasion and turned sharply to the left, swerving his tail plane clear and exposing me to the observer who was all ready. He planted a burst straight at my scout's nose! Several bullets found their mark and one removed one of my flying wires.

"This made things rather warm for me," McCall continued, having ensured the rapt attention of his audience.

"I quickly swerved to the left and jammed my throttle wide open. My wee scout lunged forward and soon brought me again in the shelter of my opponent's tail plane, having thus cut the corner. From here I kicked on the right rudder and skidded around until my gun and telescopic sight, which are on fixed mountings and are aimed by pointing the entire machine, came in line to fire.

"Taking careful aim at the centre of my opponent's machine, I pressed the two tiny levers on my control stick and brought into play my two highly efficient machine guns. There was a deafening roar of flying lead, and then I saw a puff of black smoke emerge from the enemy's cockpit. This was followed by a huge sheet of livid flame."

He stopped for a moment to take a sip from his glass, as the audience waited in suspense. He must have made it; here he was right in front of them — but how did he do it?

"Zooming to one side, I just managed to clear my scout from the explosion. Looking down, I saw the tragic mass of wreckage tearing toward the earth some 8,000 feet below, at a terrific rate of speed. Just as the machine started on its fatal plunge, I saw the observer jump overboard. Pieces of the wreckage broke off at different times during the plunge, and one flaming section landed on top of an enemy observation balloon, setting it on fire and completely destroying it. The charred metal parts, such as the engine, crashed into the ground on the bank of a canal, burying the engine, no doubt, out of sight."

The audience let out a collective sigh, but McCall's story wasn't over.

"I circled above until the crash was completed, and then turned my nose west and sped homeward as I judged that my gasoline supply was about exhausted. When I arrived at my 'drome, my machine was punctured and scarred." He smiled and shrugged. "But, with the replacement of a few parts and wires, it was none the worse for the encounter, and luckily neither was I."

News from Afar

The war hero McCall, back safely on home territory, was now like his captive audience in at least one respect. He had to depend on the newspapers or the radio to learn of the victories and tragedies being experienced by his colleagues overseas. The period of November 4–10, 1918, saw the last intense combat of the war, with the RAF suffering 60 losses to achieve a victory over the enemy, who lost 68 aircraft as a result of Allied engagement. The next morning, November 11, the crew of an RE-8 flying with No. 15 Squadron came in to Auchy to report that they could see no enemy aircraft or anti-aircraft fire. The war was over before McCall's leave was up. He would not return to the Front.

November 11 became celebrated as the anniversary of the armistice to end "The Great War" — so called because no one could believe there would ever be another of such magnitude. Like McCall's contribution, Canada's overall participation had been considerable. Over eight percent of the country's population of seven million people had signed up, sending 600,000 soldiers to the war effort, with 16,000 accepted into the air services. In fact, Canadians, fighting under the British flag, accounted for one-third of all British airmen. More than 66,000 Canucks in total made the ultimate sacrifice with their lives.

Another Kind of Victory

Many more had supported the war efforts through other avenues. It was while participating in the Victory Bond Drives that McCall met an attractive young woman who had been volunteering on the home front for the Red Cross. Freddie married Genevieve "Gen" Mullins Strong on March 26, 1919, in a quiet ceremony at her parents' home on American Hill (later called Mount Royal). The humorous newspaper headlines read, "Famous Fighting Aviator Succumbs to Barbs of L'il Dan Cupid."

Captain McCall relinquished his commission a few months later on June 23, 1919. The war had been won after all, and other things took precedence in his life. He was a hero locally, nationally, and internationally. He was a happily married man. Now to find a job.

Freddie's bride, Genevieve "Gen" Mullins Strong.

CHAPTER 5

Flying the Friendlier Skies

FREDDIE MCCALL YEARNED TO BE IN THE AIR AGAIN, AND HE WASN'T ALONE. OTHERS WHO'D RETURNED FROM OVERSEAS AERIAL COMBAT — INCLUDING THE EDMONTON WAR ACE WILFRID REID "WOP" MAY — FELT THE SAME WAY. THE TWO FLIERS REALIZED THAT MANY OTHER CANADIANS HAD BECOME ENTHRALLED WITH AVIATION DURING THE WAR. AT THE CALGARY ANNUAL EXHIBITION (THE PRECURSOR TO THE CALGARY STAMPEDE), STUNT FLYING BY CANADIAN AND AMERICAN PILOTS — IN EVERYTHING FROM DIRIGIBLES TO BIPLANES — HAD BECOME ALMOST REGULAR FEATURES. THAT WAS WHAT MCCALL AND WOP MAY WANTED TO DO: SHOW CROWDS THEIR STUNT FLYING!

Calgary area's first airstrip had come into use in 1914. Just east of Bowness Road, the grass field extended in an easterly direction for approximately one mile, or longer if needed, depending on the wind direction and speed. The Bowness Flying Field was near the electric rail line so people could come out by streetcar to watch the flying.

In the spring of 1919, Calgarian George Webber formally established the flying field with the purchase of Calgary's first commercial airplane, a "Canuck" (Canadian-built Curtiss JN-4). This was a biplane mainly used in North America during the war as a trainer aircraft. Webber built a hangar for Webber Aero Service, and hired ex-World War I pilot Lieut. Frank Donnelly to make short flights and do some exhibition flying. Webber's Canuck soon met with an accident, however. The pilot attempted a takeoff with a leaking gas pipe, which shut off the gasoline and forced a landing in a rock pile.

Undeterred, McCall travelled with Gen and Wop May to Minneapolis to evaluate a U.S.-built Curtiss JN-4D "Jenny" airplane for stunt flying. His brave wife went along on the check flight and, although Freddie put the aircraft through loop-the-loops, spinning nose dives, barrel rolls, falling leaf formations, Immelmann Turns, and vertical banks, she never batted an eye. "I hadn't gone up 50 feet the last time," McCall reported, "until Mrs. McCall was asking me to do the 'loop-the-loop.'"

STUNTING

Two Curtiss Jenny biplanes were thus acquired, disassembled, and transported back to Canada by a special railway express car to be reassembled at the Bowness Flying Field.

Wop May's "Griffon" Jenny, later to become Freddie's aircraft.

The Jennies had been covered with Irish linen and then painted with many coats of nitrate dope, leaving a finish similar to varnish, which protected the fabric from the sun and weather. May's aircraft (#34210) came decorated with a griffon on the fuselage, while McCall's (#34214) sported the profile of an Indian in full-feathered headdress on both sides of the fuselage.

The Jenny was very different from the typical WWI fighter aircraft. Fighters had short wingspans and high horsepower engines that turned small propellers at high rpm. The Jenny, on the other hand, had a relatively large wingspan – over 43 feet – and a loaded weight of 1,920 pounds. A 90-hp V-8 OX-5 engine powered a large propeller that spun at low rpm. As a result, it could achieve speeds of no more than 75 mph. Slow and forgiving of pilot errors, the Jenny was ideal for use as a trainer aircraft.

Stunt flying, however, was another matter. It took considerable flying skill to stunt with the Jenny, as its size and slow airspeed contributed to the tendency to stall and fall into an uncontrollable spin. Successful pilots had to know when the airplane was on the verge of stalling while they were carrying out dangerous stunts, and also just what action to take to keep the plane flying.

Nevertheless, both McCall and May signed contracts with Western Canadian Fair Management to do stunt flying exhibitions in the Jennies throughout Western Canada. Performing many of the aerial manoeuvres they had perfected during the war, they put on amazing exhibitions with this cumbersome aircraft.

But the intrepid wartime pilots soon discovered that the prairie landscape and climate were not ideal for these planes. The wired construction of the Curtiss JN-4Ds suffered on the rough pastures posing as airfields. The bolts of the cabane (centre upper-wing section) sometimes sheared off at the fuselage fitting, and stove-bolts were often used to repair the lost hardware. These weren't as strong as the nickel-steel bolts

Maverick in the Sky

they'd replaced, and frequently broke from the hard landings. Calgary's altitude of 3,600 feet also caused some problems for the Jenny. Because of the thin air the aircraft's performance was marginal at that altitude. The top cowl was usually left off to keep the engine from heating up, even in cool weather. As well, engines at that time were not designed to cope with Alberta's cold climate. It was common practice during winter to drain oil and water from the engines after they had been turned off; prior to start-up these fluids would then be pre-heated and replaced in the engines. Gasoline, delivered in five-gallon cans, was strained through a chamois to separate out water or dirt, and then poured into the tank by hand using a funnel.

In those days, if McCall had to fly in after dark he'd call in advance to Gen. She would then contact neighbours and friends to bring their cars out and line them along the runway, their headlights lighting the Bowness airstrip. The system may have been primitive, but it worked.

Despite the challenges, the two flying aces, McCall and May, put on exciting performances at the "A"-class fairs throughout the prairies. Soon, no fair or exhibition was considered complete without such aerial antics. Following their daily shows, the pilots would encourage the public to pay for short, thrilling rides.

When they landed in a field near a town, a crowd usually gathered and the pilots would ask, "Who would like to come for a ride?" At first it wasn't easy to convince someone to go up, so the McCalls hatched a scheme. Following a pause in response, a five-foot-tall woman in the crowd would put up her hand and shout, "I'd like to try it! I'll go!" The crowd would part to let the small woman through, amazed at her courage.

McCall would then take her up for a ride, perform some gentle stunts, and bring her back down. "Hmm, if she can do it, I can, too," many would think, and more were ready to pay $5 for a five-minute flight. The woman was, of course, Captain Freddie's wife, Gen, and the scheme worked every time.

The Town of Bowness (yet to be annexed to the City of Calgary) was certainly benefiting from its flying field, which was the first public park in Canada to have airmen as weekly attractions. On June 29, 1919, McCall arranged for a *Calgary Herald* staff photographer named Bill Oliver to take the first aerial photos of the City of Calgary. The little airstrip was also the delivery point for the first merchandise ever to be shipped to Calgary by air. It became the midpoint of the first double-crossing of the Rocky Mountains (by Captain Ernest C. Hoy, DFC, in August 1919 in a Curtiss JN-4), and also provided the final stopover for the first trans-Canada air flight (Halifax to Vancouver).

Bowness residents enjoyed close-up views of all these antics. At one time, when an out-of-town aircraft ran out of gas, local children went running over to see who, or what, might emerge from the machine. "A man from Mars would not have seemed more strange," one person recalled. Now, airplanes and those who flew and fixed them were common sights and much admired.

CALGARY'S FIRST FLYING CLUB

The best way to get more people interested in flying and to encourage pilot training, Capt. McCall reasoned, was to form an organized flying club. In June of 1919 the Calgary Aero Club was launched, with Lieut. S.J. (Sam) Lee as president, Capt. McCall as first vice-president, and 49 other like-minded charter members. As one of the club's most famous and maverick fliers, McCall was expected to enhance its membership drive by enticing equally well-known, but better-financed, Calgary businessmen to become honorary members.

Pat Burns was McCall's first, and much-publicized, "target". The well-liked owner of the successful P. Burns and Company was acknowledged as "Alberta's Cattle King", and lived in a mansion at 4th Street between 12th and 13th Avenues. On the morning of July 3, 1919, McCall set off for these coordinates in his Curtiss JN-4D.

He circled the Burns mansion and then dived out of a half-roll to plummet to 100 feet above its roof. Circling low to give his passenger, Lieut. Percy Payne, a former air force navigator, time to step out onto a wing, McCall descended to just above the telephone wires. Payne dropped a 20-pound leather-wrapped "bomb" close to the target before climbing back inside the aircraft. McCall then did some stunt flying over the estate, to the delight of the crowd that had gathered below.

Hearing the noise of the airplane, Pat Burns's son Michael ran outside to see the object bouncing onto their spacious, groomed grounds. He recognized "the bomber" immediately, laughed, and waved as McCall flew off. Inside the "bomb" package was an invitation for honorary membership in the Calgary Aero Club. The gambit was successful and Pat Burns accepted the nomination.

A MEMORABLE RIDE

In 1919, the Calgary Exhibition's brand new grandstand gave crowds spectacular views of the takeoffs, stunts, and landings of Alberta's flying heroes McCall and May. The annual celebrations began with McCall swooping in to land — virtually at the feet of the crowd — to bring in the VIP who would open the fair. The *Calgary Herald's* headlines were as spectacular as the flights: "Curving, Twisting, Diving Airplane Carries Gen. H.F. McDonald to Exhibition — Captain Fred McCall brings spectators' hearts into their throats as he puts the big Curtiss machine through daring evolutions." Only a few exhibition patrons seemed unappreciative, querulously complaining that McCall's low flying had blown off their hats.

Another thrilling stunt at the Calgary Stampede was racing with famous car drivers Barney Oldfield and Bill Endicott in the infield, against McCall in the air in the Jenny. Added to the fabulous mix of entertainment was a full musical presentation by John Phillip Sousa, one of the world's top bandmasters, and his 55-member band.

1919 Calgary Exhibition poster featuring barnstormers McCall and May.

Maverick in the Sky

Freddie with Barney Oldfield, auto racer.

On July 5 of that same year, McCall strapped two young passengers into the front seat of his open cockpit to give them an aerial view of the Stampede events. Herbert, age 13, and his brother Ronald, age 11, were the sons of the Calgary Exhibition Manager, Ernest L. Richardson. They were thrilled to be flying over the crowds, viewing the midway rides and races. McCall usually started eastward from the west end of the field. This time, because of winds, he took off from the centre field in the opposite direction. The Jenny rose 200 feet in the air, and then suddenly its engine sputtered and died. Since the automobile race was already underway, it was impossible to return and land on the infield. There was no clear spot on the crowded midway either. Dropping the tail to give the aircraft the necessary impetus to lift over the racetrack and clear the fence, McCall's wheels caught a telephone wire. Down came the wires and pole.

Freddie's parents and sister, Marjorie, along with a crowd of thousands, watched in horror as the powerless aircraft hung in the air, tripped on the wires, and then headed downwards in a long glide. McCall looked down, his mind racing

Capt. McCall taking off in the Jenny from the Calgary Exhibition infield, July 5, 1919.

through rapid calculations of flight and glide. There was only one choice left. His precise combat flying skills produced a split-second reflex action: he expertly stalled the aircraft onto the wide canvas-covered top of the merry-go-round. There perched the Jenny, on a tilt, with the centre pole of the ride puncturing the floor of the aircraft and protruding vertically between the two boys.

Fair-goers stared up in shock, and then rushed forward to rescue the pilot and passengers, even as announcer Alex Sloane tried to calm them by repeating that the accident was slight and no one was injured. This was true, but the incredible flight, stall, and landing were caught on film and immortalized. Amazingly, it was McCall's first post-war forced landing — and it became renowned as the world's most astonishing air accident. Later, McCall reasoned what had happened: some-

Maverick in the Sky

Forced landing on carousel due to engine failure shortly after take-off.

one in the front cockpit had accidentally touched the throttle, cutting off the power.

Once the Jenny was lowered to the ground, people clamoured for souvenirs. When some ladies took off their high-heeled shoes to whack at the wrecked aircraft's fabric covering, the midway manager had an idea. He draped a tent over the Jenny, opened a booth, and charged each person 25 cents to come in and take a look, and even rip off a small piece of fabric as a memento of this miraculous controlled landing. He then split the profits with McCall.

"Why don't you do the same at Edmonton's Big Victory Fair?" suggested Wop May. So the Jenny was shipped north by rail, and admissions collected there as well. A wing walker, and a novice parachutist added by May and McCall in Edmonton, attracted more notice to the amazing feat of flight. When the young man initially expressed a slight fear of parachuting, McCall quickly assured him that "parachutes open nine times out of 10." The parachutist jumped nine times, then quit.

These ventures raised sufficient funds to replace the aircraft, and Calgary's flying ace was soon in the air again.

The time had come, however, for flying machines to be used for more than just thrill-seeking rides and exhibitions. Indeed, aircraft were soon destined to play ever-increasing roles in the fields of commerce and exploration. Freddie McCall would once again be at the forefront.

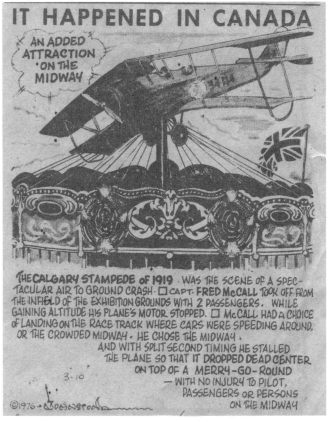

Freddie McCall's miraculous carousel landing attracted attention around the world.

Maverick in the Sky

CHAPTER 6
"Business" Flights

THE *ALBERTAN'S* HEADLINE ON JULY 15, 1919, SHOCKED THE PUBLIC, PARTICULARLY THE FLIERS WHO HAD BEEN MAKING THEIR LIVING PROVIDING AERIAL ENTERTAINMENT: "GOVERNMENT WILL STOP STUNT FLYING NOW. DANGEROUS FLYING OVER CITIES TO BE PROHIBITED; ALSO THRILLING EXHIBITION FLIGHTS." THE PENALTIES FOR LOW-LEVEL STUNTS, OR DROPPING "DANGEROUS" ADVERTISING ITEMS FROM AIRCRAFT, RANGED FROM SIX MONTHS IN JAIL TO A FINE OF $1,000 — FOR BOTH THE PILOT AND THE OWNER OF THE MACHINE.

In June 1919, the Canada Air Board had set federal regulations for aerial activity. Rules now covered everything from licensing private pilots, flying clubs, and airline companies, to the routes and aircraft they flew. "Air Regs", as they were commonly known, became the mantra of governments and often the dirge of owners and fliers, especially mavericks who were used to taking risks and operating independently.

McCall decided it was time to get into the *business* of flying. With the money from his wrecked Jenny and financial assistance from Charles Beeching, who also became McCall's first flying student, he bought Wop May's Jenny, and took over George Webber's hangar.

LONGER FLIGHTS

On September 4, 1919, McCall again made headlines by pioneering the first cross-country flight in his new Curtiss JN-4D. The flight plan took them 70 miles south from the Bowness Flying Field to Nanton to view passenger Charles Beeching's ranch from the air. En route they dropped papers over the Town of High River to advertise an upcoming show

— thus launching Calgary's first airmail delivery, and the first commercial air flight in Southern Alberta.

When McCall later flew to Nanton for its Field Day, he took with him his apprentice air engineer, Roland Murray, who faithfully recorded memories of that 45-minute trip: the long taxi run almost to the railway tracks, rapid takeoff, and climb to an altitude of 2,000–3,000 feet; and the breathtaking scene of the Bow River Valley below, with Calgary visible six miles to the east. He also reported the detour they made over the pilot's home so Gen McCall would know they were on their way. McCall and Murray followed along the Canadian Pacific Railway line to the west, with the snow-capped Rockies in one window and the flat prairie land in the other, "stretching eastward to infinity," and in all colours — from the black summer fallow to green pastureland and golden-ripe fields of grain.

Murray was along not only as a passenger but also as a mechanic, and did not neglect to describe the airplane itself in his trip record. The Curtiss OX-5 engine had a peculiar valve action system. The valve rocker arms protruded through the top of the engine and their action could be seen from the front cockpit. "As the valve gear always has to run at half engine speed on four-cycle engines, the action was so slow I could almost see the rocker arms stop at the bottom and top of their strokes. There were three arms on the top of each cylinder. The long rocker arm was pivoted at its centre, while the two short ones were rotated up and down on the same shaft at its ends. There were two dozen of these busy little fellows bouncing up and down out front in the 60-miles-per-hour breeze, and they were very intriguing to watch."

Meanwhile, McCall was busy listening. The wires hummed and whined as he throttled back the motor to glide in for a landing. If the whine began to die out, McCall knew he was flying too slowly. If he didn't push the nose down to gain speed, the wings would stall and the airplane would dive until it picked up enough speed to start flying again. Listening to the wires was also crucial to knowing the aircraft speed when performing various aerobatic manoeuvres.

As Nanton came into view, they descended to 200 feet over the town. Murray looked over the left side of the airplane to see a horse-drawn buggy coming along one of the streets. Its driver leaned over to look up at the airplane, obviously shocked by the contrast between these two modes of travel.

McCall landed in a soft ploughed field, only later admitting that it was risky for a nose-over. As they tied down the aircraft to prevent it from taking off in the wind, people started to gather. That day he took 35 people up for rides. Even Nanton's mayor happily went up. McCall took off down the field to the west, climbed to 1,000 feet while turning slowly to the south, made a circuit, and then turned around to land and taxi back to the take-off point.

While the aviators ate the lunch that the townsfolk had brought them, they kept the engine running. Suddenly everything was too quiet. They looked up to see the aircraft moving off slowly down the field, propelled by the wind. Roland Murray caught up to it first, and quickly clambered up to the lower wing and reached into the cockpit to close the throttle. They then had to fly home before dark, with the vision of the setting sun behind the Rockies presenting a final spectacle at the close of a memorable day.

These trips were so successful that McCall continued to visit small towns in Southern Alberta, flying west to Cochrane, or east to Rosedale near Drumheller, southwest to Bassano, Gleichen, Brooks, Medicine Hat, and Taber, and again south from Calgary to Blackie, Vulcan, High River, Nanton, and Claresholm. He was in the air again, and getting paid for it.

McCall's exploits continued to be the talk of the town. On September 12, 1919, he was flying with a company member when they hit a Canada goose at 75 miles per hour. Roland Murray reported: "The goose hit one of the wires of the wing truss and was thrown into the front cockpit, knocking Capt. Brett out cold, and then it fell over the side of the aeroplane."

As McCall started to make preparations to land to get first aid, his co-pilot recovered consciousness and so they continued on home to Bowness. The only damage to the aircraft was a small nick in one propeller blade.

ROYAL BUZZ

On September 13, 1919, McCall formed his first company, McCall Aero Corporation.

A few days later, he and a friend were flying along the Bow River when they spotted a passenger train. McCall decided it might be fun to "buzz" the train, and swooped down to roar alongside the cars at window level. McCall's flying was expert, his demeanour charming, and his nerve astounding. He made several passes, enjoying the open-mouthed stares of the rail passengers.

Capt. McCall receives his Distinguished Service Order (DSO) in Calgary from the visiting Prince of Wales.

On that particular day, there happened to be a very important person on that train. The Prince of Wales was on his way back from a visit to Vancouver to his EP Ranch south of Calgary. Ironically, during his stopover, one of his royal duties was to present Capt. McCall with the Distinguished Service Order he had earned but not yet received because he had been

Maverick in the Sky

sent home early from the Front. The Palliser Hotel, often called The Paralyzer, hosted a fine event that night. There was an even finer party afterwards as the Prince was known to enjoy a tipple or two, especially with a pilot audacious enough to "buzz" the Royal train.

McCall continued to visit various towns in the "Griffon" Jenny (now registered as G-CAAH, the "G" standing for Great Britain and "C" for Canada.). On September 18, he flew 20 miles west along the Bow River to Cochrane and was caught in such a sudden gale that the aircraft seemed to descend vertically. Nonetheless, several days later he flew over the mountains to Nelson, B.C., to give a stunting exhibition at their fair, and then on to Cranbrook to do the same there.

Flying in to these mountain-ringed towns that were subject to ever-changing wind currents was not easy. There were no wheel brakes on airplanes in 1919, and the aviator almost needed a second person's help if he wished to make a sharp turn at very low speed. Otherwise, the aircraft always wanted to head into the wind. The rudder had to be held over to one side and the motor run at almost full power to help blow the tail to the other side. But McCall, always up for a challenge, thought the mountain residents deserved a good air show.

On October 2, 1919, McCall flew his first cross-country female passenger, Willa V. Coultry of Okotoks, to Shorty McLaughlan's farm west of High River. She later published an article in a Vancouver magazine that recalled the "mad rush" at takeoff, the thrill of the ground "seeming to drop away" beneath them, the noise of the aircraft in flight, and the extreme beauty of the scenery.

Another of McCall's female passengers, Edna Jaques, published a poem following her memorable airplane trip with McCall.

The wind sings loud in our pulsing ears
As we rush through that boundless space,
We feel the hot touch of wind-whipped tears
And their salty sting in our face . . .

Like a soul set free from its prison chains
Must pause in its upward flight,
And looking down to the earth again
Sees life in its perfect light.

The fame of Calgary's World War I flying ace's peacetime endeavours was spreading throughout Canada's West, as his flying activities continued into late fall. The Hudson's Bay Company store had hired local pilots to drop souvenir streamers over the town to advertise its 249th anniversary. One of McCall's "hangar rats", 12-year-old Jim Dolan, remembers that one of his oddest jobs was to fill 20 balloons with buckshot pellets, and blow them up to the size of coconuts. The balloons were then released from the cockpit of the Curtiss Jenny, and eagerly grabbed by children at store company picnics. Since some of the balloons contained tickets for prizes, a few children even plunged into the lagoon in pursuit of the precious objects.

SANTA CLAUS IS FLYING TO TOWN . . .

Coming into the Christmas season, the Hudson's Bay Company then booked McCall to fly Santa Claus over Calgary. Lights were installed on the Jenny's wingtips so they could be seen in the dark. The event was sensational, but landing the aircraft in the dark proved to be a problem. Gasoline torches had been laid out and lit, but from the air they were difficult to differentiate from the town's lights. Even though McCall let down slowly, he ended up being a good distance from the intended landing place. The rough landing also snapped both tips off the propeller.

Hearing the roar of the engine and the whine of the broken propeller, mechanic Roland Murray started a few more signal fires to guide McCall back to the hangar. He then ran out to meet the aircraft, which had made it only part way down the field. They put out the fires and got a car to tow the aircraft up to the hangar.

Daylight revealed that one end of the propeller had gone through the leading edge of the upper port wing. Having determined that there was no damage to the front spar or any other part of the primary structure, they cut up a five-gallon gasoline can, wrapped part of it around the broken wooden leading edge, and fastened it in place. Then they doped some fabric over the patch and painted it — good as new.

Despite the accident, the publicity created by the Santa Claus stunt proved that "the going up was worth the coming down." With such activities bringing in revenue to the tune of about $600 per day, the McCall Aero Corporation was encouraged to order three Canucks from the Ericson Company in Toronto for the following spring.

On November 6, 1919, the Calgary Aero Club held a convention in Calgary to form a cross-Canada organization. Chaired by McCall and attended by local as well as federal government representatives, it helped form the Canadian Air Service Association that would prove critical to Canadian airline development. McCall was elected president.

McCall's personal life was evolving just as rapidly. With the birth of daughter Geraldine "Gerrie" Virginia McCall on January 6, 1920, he became a father. The family was by then living on 17th Avenue West. The McCall family — children, dogs, and all — was destined to move often, always renting, and never owning their own home.

AIRLINE BUSINESS

Making a steady living in aviation was becoming increasingly difficult. In Canada and the U.S., people with much deeper pockets than McCall were getting into aviation activity, and making progress well beyond stunt-flying, five-dollars-a-head circuits over local fairs, or short passenger hops. As competition accelerated, business ventures were always starting up, folding, and restarting.

In Edmonton, McCall's friend Wop May and his pilot brother Court were still doing stunt shows in a Curtiss Jenny with Wop's famous name painted on the top of the aircraft so spectators could see it when he was flying upside down. Their work also expanded to aerial photography, and business was so good that the brothers formed a company offering flights to destinations in central and northern Alberta.

Although he and Wop May remained friends throughout their lives, McCall chose to pursue a different aviation business than northern bush flying. McCall's dream was to establish a scheduled airline in southern Alberta, with a route from Calgary south to Lethbridge, southwest to the B.C. points of Fernie and Cranbrook, and back through Banff to Calgary. He also hoped to gain the financial security of an airmail service route, particularly through the difficult mountainous terrain west of Calgary that often kept its residents isolated. "The Rockies will present little obstacle to the development of Canada's east-west air service," McCall predicted.

But establishing a scheduled service did prove difficult. People lacked the money for individual passenger fares, and cargo transport was different from the North where the Mays were operating, which had neither bus nor train service. The South had many transportation choices, most of them a lot cheaper than shipping or travelling by air. Securing a mail route was critical and there was much lobbying in Ottawa to gain airmail franchises, which could ensure the success of a fledgling airline.

By the summer of 1920, McCall was actively seeking all types of work for his "fleet of modern aeroplanes at our well-located aerodrome at Bowness." The rate of $30 for the "Sun-down Air Trail" would take passengers on 30-mile trips over foothills and prairie, "with a never-to-be-forgotten view of the Rockies." Just $10 would buy a shorter "Observation Flight."

Commercial licences were eventually required in order to set up a public passenger service, and McCall, Canada's Number 5 air ace, was issued Commercial Licence Number 5 from Ottawa on July 31, 1920 – a fitting coincidence.

Optimistically, McCall Aero Corporation enlarged its hangar and built a new door to accommodate the three Ca-

Freddie McCall flew A.B. King from Okotoks to Black Diamond in May 1920 to conduct banking business.

nucks ordered from Toronto the previous fall. These two-seater Canadian-made aircraft were lighter than the U.S. "Jennies" and had a better lateral control system. Two were assembled at Bowness Flying Field (registered as G-CABN and G-CABO), with one retained for a spare (very likely sold soon after, as no mention of its registration could be found). McCall then hired pilots Frank Donnelly and Jack Fraser.

Finally, the Calgary Aero Club's flying school got underway, fulfilling another of McCall's dreams as he trained a number of pilots himself at the Bowness Flying Field. The Canucks, with their "very forgiving" handling characteristics, were the perfect trainer aircraft. If a pilot made a bad landing, he usually got through it all right, or at the very least the aircraft was often repairable afterward.

Despite McCall's optimism and a favourable climate that promised well for his new business, there were numerous setbacks that clouded the outlook for the fledgling enterprise. On June 6, pilot Frank Donnelly had made a forced landing in G-CABN at Rockyford, a hamlet east of Calgary. He tore through a fence and poked the nose of the aircraft into the front door of the Roman Catholic Church. No one was hurt, and the aircraft was repaired. But unfortunately, the very next month the same Canuck was damaged again — this time, beyond repair.

The second Canuck, G-CABO, was also damaged beyond repair a month later, on August 10, while being flown by Jack Fraser. Although no one was hurt in these crashes, they were severe blows to the business — and to the public's perception of aviation safety. By the end of the season, McCall's U.S.-built Jenny (G-CAAH) was the only plane he had left.

CHAPTER 7

Air and Ground Action

Despite the "Air Regs" cautioning against, and in some cases even forbidding, aerial antics, exhibitions continued to include races between automobiles and airplanes, and wing-walking and midair aircraft-changing stunts. McCall decided to step up his own show.

In the summer of 1920, he hired local wing-walker Alf Mabee. Hanging onto the flying wires of McCall's plane, Alf walked along the lower wing. His stunts on the upper wing were much more difficult. To prevent his plummeting to the ground, a type of harness was attached to the upper wing at dead centre, which Alf held on to as he performed his high-wire feats. These performances were so popular with Calgarians that the pair performed at other towns throughout the autumn.

Even more spectacular were occasional performances when McCall and Wop May flew side by side and Alf would transfer from one airplane to another. Their wings alarmingly close, one would fly slightly higher than the other and at relatively slow speeds of 60–65 mph. Still, it looked like scary stuff to the audience on the ground. And then, when the spectators thought they'd seen it all, the wing-walker would dangle by his hands or knees from the ground loop suspended beneath the lower wing.

Unintentional Stunt Flying

Gen McCall still regularly accompanied Freddie to western air shows and on his cross-country flights. She enjoyed flying with her husband, or at least she did until the day she was talked into accompanying him on a flight to Edmonton to attend a Rotarians' event.

Freddie hadn't planned to go, but their friends beseeched them to join the wonderful party at the Hotel Macdonald. By the fourth phone call, Freddie finally gave in, and he and Gen went out to the airport to start up the recently overhauled Jenny.

Gen, as passenger, climbed into the front cockpit. Almost immediately she realized that something was amiss: there were no seatbelts. She called out to Freddie, but he was already in the rear cockpit, controlling the throttle and magneto switch to start the engine while someone outside was busy spinning the prop. She looked frantically for the speaking tube to tell him the problem — but it was missing also. She then realized the terrible truth — the aircraft had not been fully re-equipped since its servicing.

Sitting in an open cockpit aircraft, as insecure as if perched on a kitchen chair, she heard and felt the rumble of the engine. The Jenny began to taxi down the runway. As they became airborne, there was nothing she could do but try to quell her fear and endure the ride. At least they would be flying straight to Edmonton, a 200-mile trip, and landing at the airport. She could just hunch low in the seat, hang on, and hope they didn't encounter a storm or rough air.

When they reached Edmonton, however, Freddie decided to give their friends at the Hotel Macdonald a good show. Circling around the third floor of the big hotel above the banks of the North Saskatchewan River, he quickly succeeded in getting their attention. The party-goers gathered at the windows, waving and hoisting their glasses in greeting. So then, just for laughs, Freddie inverted the aircraft.

Gen was not laughing. With the earth swirling below, she tucked her feet as far as possible under the instrument panel for the little security that offered, and tightly grasped the inter-plane struts that held up the small cabane wing over the open cockpit in an effort to stay in the aircraft. Freddie's show finally and mercifully ended, and he landed at Blatchford Field. A shaken and angry Gen McCall crawled out of the cockpit. "Freddie McCall, I will never fly with you again!" she said. And she never did.

The story was passed down through the years. Freddie son, Fred, wasn't born until 1928, but he heard this and other wild stories of this historic decade from relatives and other Calgarians. "You've got to remember that when these men came back from the war they were pretty traumatized, and they did a lot of partying. They were extremely popular. You come back as a national hero and everybody wants to take you here and there. The height of Dad's post-war flying career was during the roaring '20s. Life was really fast in those days, and that was their era."

UPS BUT MOSTLY DOWNS

But, for all the interest in aviation, local business was slowing down alarmingly. There just seemed no way to make money from it. By the spring of 1921, McCall Aero Corporation had sold or leased its remaining asset, the "Griffon" Jenny that McCall had purchased from Wop May (G-CAAH). While being flown by its new owner, Captain Fleming, the Jenny crashed at Bowness on June 12, 1921. Wing-walker Alf Mabee, a passenger in the front seat, was killed. A combination of unfortunate events had caused the engine to stall, and the Court of Inquiry attributed fault to both pilot error and mechanical problems. It became Calgary's first fatal air accident — a dubious honour.

During its tenure, McCall Aero Corporation had completed 685 flights and carried 674 passengers. It had flown just over 240 hours, compared to 279.50 hours McCall had flown in combat during the war!

In the spring of 1921, McCall brought in Lester Hanrahan as a partner and formed McCall Hanrahan Aero Service. They ordered a modified Avro 548 from the Canadian Aircraft Company Ltd. in Winnipeg. The day following its assembly at Bowness Field, McCall's new partner suffered such a severe bump on his nose from the rough operation of the aircraft that he spent two days in the hospital.

The oddball three-seater Avro had been rebuilt from a two-seater. The seats were set in tandem, with the result that the tail-plane bolts had to be raised or lowered to attain proper balance for the load. "Neglecting this lengthy and tedious job soon led to the end of this aeroplane," lamented mechanic Roland Murray.

The Avro (G-CACN) was partially wrecked in its first week of operation, rebuilt the next, and then, a month later, wrecked for good when McCall had to abort a takeoff near Ardenode, north of Strathmore. Although there were no injuries, the accident was enough to end the company. McCall Hanrahan Aero Service had flown only seven hours and completed only seven flights — no lucky sevens for McCall.

More resilient than his airplanes, McCall had meanwhile formed a new company, adding another partner. McCall-Hanrahan-Bennet Aeroplanes Limited was incorporated on June 27, 1921, and assumed the (almost zero) assets of Mc-Call Hanrahan Aero Service. But, with few resources and no work, the company was virtually inactive and was eventually struck from the register on May 30, 1925.

Reluctantly, McCall felt it was time to give up on aviation, at least for a while. In 1922, he went to work as an electrician for Gauge and Coyle Mining Company in Drumheller — a rather extreme change for an airman to be underground for eight to 10 hours a day! He'd come home covered with coal dust, exhausted and discouraged, but with a wife and child to support he stuck it out for two years. While McCall's next job didn't take him into the air either, at least he was above ground, this time as a vendor for the Alberta Liquor Control Board. It was an easier job but still not one he was born to do.

CHAPTER 8

Daring Adventures

When the Calgary Aero Club had finally re-established in 1927, McCall was elected president, and was again determined to promote its activities and growth in any way he could. He was a dynamic speaker, and still carried the aura of an aviation hero. At the first meeting of the club, held in the Mewata Armories, over 100 members were convinced to sign up for ground-school instruction, and more than 30 for actual flying lessons. McCall was initially one of the instructors. This show of interest, and the fact that the club had a licensed flying instructor and an engineer (George Hoskin), had enabled it to apply for a federal government grant for two DeHavilland 60X Cirrus Moths. Freddie and the boys of the Aero Club had exciting plans for the two Moths.

Purple Plane

Freddie returned to employment in the aviation industry in March of 1928 as chief pilot with a newly formed company.

Purple Label Airline Ltd. was owned by Emil Sick of Associated Breweries of Canada Ltd. and ignominiously named after one of their beer labels. The company's first acquisition was a Stinson SB-1 Detroiter (registered as G-CANI).

McCall and co-pilot Jock Palmer were sent to Detroit to take possession of the new biplane. While they were waiting for the bright purple paint to be applied, the area was hit by a snowstorm. No problem, McCall thought, if the weather was bad in one direction, he would simply choose a different flight path. It might take a little longer, but it wasn't a big deal. During the zigzag trip home, Freddie sent telegrams to Gen, regularly apprising her of their current location. In Winnipeg, owner Emil Sick joined the pilots and the *Calgary Herald* reporter who was along for the ride and the story.

Running out of gas at Medicine Hat caused another delay because they had to wait for fuel to be shipped by rail. The 25-hour trip from Detroit was finally completed on April 29, 1928, when they swooped in to land at Bowness Field. The Stinson had been the talk of the town and caused an immediate reaction from a cheering crowd who'd gathered to greet it. Aside from its shocking colour, it was the first passenger aircraft to have a fully enclosed cabin. It could accommodate four passengers and two crewmembers, or could carry over a ton of freight, and cruise at 100 miles per hour.

The aircraft had a longer life than the airline that owned it, however. The assets of Purple Label Airline Ltd. were soon turned over to Great Western Airways Ltd. (GWA), formed on May 22, 1928, and also owned by Emil Sick. Capt. McCall became both the managing director and chief pilot.

PRANKS

When the Bowness Flying Field was declared unfit because of erratic winds and other problems, the Calgary Aero Club and other flying companies had to temporarily relocate. In August 1928 the club levelled a new field for the Banff Coach Road Aerodrome and raised money for hangars. At the club's first air show at the new location on September 29, 1928, Freddie's wife Gen christened the Aero Club's two new Moths (G-CALA and G-GAKQ) with champagne. A large crowd had gathered to watch pilots Freddie McCall, W.L. Rutledge, and Jock Palmer perform. This show was intended to be so spectacular it would convince even more Calgarians to sign up for memberships and lessons.

McCall took off in a Moth, blowing up dust as he roared over the heads of the spectators, heading north toward the Nose Creek valley at the far end of the field. But suddenly the aircraft started to wobble, and then lurch drunkenly over

Winter flying. Freddie in front of Great West Airways D.H. 60X Cirrus Moth. Aircraft named "Kit" in honour of owner Emil Sick's wife.

the brow of the hill. To the people watching, it seemed certain to crash on the far side of the hill or down on the railway tracks! What a terrible way to convince people to join the Aero Club!

The crowd waited anxiously, many covering their ears and eyes in dread. Would their war hero really hit the dirt at an air show, after all he'd been through overseas? There *had* been a lot of crashes lately.

A plume of black smoke suddenly rose from the valley. An ambulance and fire engine thundered across the field and screeched to a stop at the top of the hill. The crews jumped out and disappeared over the horizon. Then they came back to stop beside their vehicles, gesturing among themselves, as if in total confusion. As one man looked up and pointed to the sky, everyone heard a tremendous roar.

McCall's aircraft zoomed into view from the north. The Moth swooped so low that its wheels touched the hangar roof and clipped the windsock. Freddie executed a right turn that almost pivoted a wingtip on the ground, and he then dropped to land. The aircraft rolled to a stop and the pilot disembarked to join the incredulous crowd and await the return of the empty ambulance and fire engine.

McCall later explained that he'd nosed his aircraft over the brow of the hill into the valley and then, when out of sight, had banked and flown up Nose Creek. He'd climbed out of the valley, turned into the wind, and then raced back to the airfield to beat the emergency crew. But the smoke? "Oh," he said, with a sly grin, "a couple of fellows were stationed down there in the valley, to set fire to an oil drum."

A Stinson Detroiter, circa 1930.

At some shows, McCall carried the gags even further. He'd have the Moth sitting outside the hangar with the engine running. McCall's brother-in-law, Gordon Ross, was a sports broadcaster for CJCJ radio, and also the air show announcer. Ross would call the audience's attention to the aircraft sitting empty out on the field, with the prop turning, and then he would excitedly announce, "Oh my gosh! There's a little old lady walking over to that airplane!"

Indeed, there she was, in her dress and hat and swinging her purse as she tottered up to the Moth. "Lady, come away from that airplane! It's dangerous!" Ross would cry. And when she climbed into the airplane anyway, "Oh, what are you doing? Please, get out of that airplane! Somebody stop her!" Ross continued to plead.

The cockpit door closed, and the aircraft lurched and then took off in a crazy wobble. Away it went, up in the air, over the horizon and into the valley. And suddenly there was the dreaded plume of black smoke. "I can't believe it," Ross wailed. "Ladies and gentlemen, we've just witnessed a terrible tragedy! That old lady has just crashed the airplane!"

"Oh my God, this is terrible! She's killed herself!" mourned people in the crowd, shielding their children's eyes from the terrible sight as the ambulance and fire engine raced to the rescue.

And then, from the opposite direction from where the aircraft had gone down, back it came, barely 10 feet off the ground, to zoom overhead! People ducked, afraid that this crazy woman would kill them all.

Finally the Moth came in to land. As it rolled to a stop, officials raced to open the door to help the nutty old lady disembark. She brushed off their help, gingerly stepped down, and then ran, laughing, over to the audience, removing her hat and waving it in the air. The little old lady was, of course, Capt. Freddie McCall.

These air shows were unequalled successes, and McCall's status as a magical and enchanting flier and showman was proven over and over again.

MEMORABLE OCCASIONS

The Aero Club booked its first annual general meeting, to include a fancy fundraising dinner and membership drive, in the elegant Palliser Hotel. McCall decided it would encourage people to attend if one of the club's aircraft was brought inside and set up as a display behind the head table.

The crew struggled to get one of the club's new Cirrus Moths up the front steps of the Palliser but, even with its wings folded, the hotel's revolving doors presented a problem. They went around the back to try and take it up the freight elevator. Alas, it wouldn't fit. The solution was to lower the elevator so its roof was even with the floor, remove the prop, and wheel in the Moth, nose down and wings folded, onto the top of the elevator. Using this unorthodox method, they manoeuvred the 1,000-pound aircraft inside and triumphantly wheeled it into the Crystal Ballroom. They set it up on a stage behind the head table, unfolded the wings, and reattached the propeller.

Everything was going fine, and attendees were duly impressed to see the aircraft so well displayed. But that wasn't enough for Freddie McCall, especially after he'd sipped on a couple of highballs. These folks deserved the real thing!

He jumped into the cockpit and called for a helper to spin the prop. It sputtered and died. When he tried it again, the same thing happened. McCall kept adding more throttle. The engine suddenly caught and roared to life, belching out a cloud of intense blue smoke that completely filled the room. Oil had run into the cylinders when the aircraft was tipped up for its ride on the elevator. The result was an intense and choking stench that drove the attendees for the door, and left the Crystal Ballroom with ruined walls and draperies.

The stunt attracted the publicity that McCall and the Aero Club wanted, but not the kind of publicity that the Palliser Hotel needed. However, no one who attended that first annual general meeting ever forgot it.

A personally memorable event to close the year of 1928 was the birth of a son to Freddie and Gen McCall. Fred Robert (never called Fred Junior) was born in the Scottish Nursing Home in Calgary at 6 p.m. on Christmas Eve. When Freddie was informed of his son's arrival, he immediately got together with some of his cronies to celebrate — and Gen didn't see him for two days. However, she received a dozen roses every hour on the hour, until the Nursing Home complained that they couldn't cope and asked Freddie to desist! The little family was now complete. With the arrival of his son and the new aircraft, McCall's fortunes seemed assured.

MORE THAN STUNTS

McCall's aviation career broke new ground with the arrival of the Stinson Detroiter. On January 19, 1929, he flew the Stinson to Banff, landing on the frozen Bow River. The purpose was to prove the feasibility of opening a commercial air route, with Banff as one of the landing sites.

Late that Saturday afternoon, the roar of an aircraft engine was heard over the Banff town site, as McCall brought the Stinson Detroiter in to land on the ice of the Bow River. Typical of McCall's pioneering efforts, it was a risky endeavour and very nearly came to grief. First, the aircraft bumped the pontoon bridge. Quickly taking to the air again, it flew on for a few more feet to touch the ice with the tail to one side.

First Banff landing. RCMP officer and pilot Freddie McCall standing in front of Stinson Detroiter on frozen Bow River.

No one had ever landed an aircraft in Banff before and the *Banff Crag and Canyon* newspaper excitedly chronicled this inaugural event: "Landing in this position, the plane started to skid and it was only through skilful piloting that it was manoeuvred from hitting the boathouse on the river, although the tail skid did catch the boardwalk around the building, but did no particular damage."

Capt. McCall alighted from the aircraft, accompanied by his Calgary passengers Dr. Jack Hesson and Clinton Adams, and Banff passenger William McCardell, to great fanfare. A party was held, of course, and to commemorate the occasion the Banff Winter Carnival Association presented Freddie with a sterling silver baby mug, suitably engraved, to be given to his son Fred, now all of four weeks old.

The takeoff the next afternoon gave the crowd — and McCall's passengers, who now included Norman K. Luxton of Banff — a performance just as interesting, and dangerous, as the landing. A strong breeze had begun to blow, and it caught the aircraft just as it left the ice and whirled it over to the right upstream bank of the river. Fortunately, this was at the point where Echo Creek empties into the Bow River.

"With considerable presence of mind, Capt. McCall turned the plane's nose up this stream, and for about 500 yards dodged trees in this narrow lane until he gained altitude. Had it not been for the fortunate position of this creek, the plane would have in all likelihood crashed into the tree-lined bank of the Bow River," stated the *Banff Crag and Canyon*.

The trip back to Calgary, with the aircraft boosted by the wind, was made in the record time of 38 minutes. The Luxton Museum of Banff proudly added a unique display to its usual exhibits — the tip of a fir tree clipped off by the Stinson's landing gear during McCall's takeoff.

Following the success of this inaugural trip, Great Western Airways immediately began offering $15 one-way flights from Calgary to Banff for passengers wishing to attend the winter carnival.

McCall followed this feat by pioneering a loop service that included Calgary, Banff, Fernie, Lethbridge, and Medicine Hat, making a round trip over some of the most rugged mountainous flying country in the world. On February 15, he made further headlines by flying from Lethbridge to Calgary in a record 55 minutes, with three passengers.

The intrepid flier was intent on demonstrating aviation's multiple uses, and in February 1929, the newspapers reported that McCall had performed a rescue flight by transporting the injured son of a certain Mrs. MacLaren from Skiff, Alberta, to the hospital in Lethbridge. This, it was noted, had changed Mrs. MacLaren's opinion about the value of air transport, which she had apparently disparaged before.

But on February 22 and 23, 1929, McCall made the most incredible flights of all in the Stinson Detroiter. Calmont Oils Ltd. of Calgary had announced that it planned to "shoot" the company's latest oil drilling venture in Turner Valley with nitro-glycerine in an effort to bring a reluctant well into production. The explosive was manufactured in Shelby, Montana, but the railway refused to carry such dangerous material. Even if the nitro wasn't considered too high a risk for ground transport, the roads had become so heavily drifted with snow that they were nearly impassable for trucks. Ferrying the explosives by air seemed the only solution.

Great Western Airways was hired for the job, with Fred McCall as the intrepid pilot. He would be flying 250 miles each way in zero-degree weather, and landing on the snow-covered fields of the Banff Coach Road Aerodrome. A hard landing risked an explosion, so they required the permission of the Controller of Civil Aviation.

McCall was accompanied by Charles B. Stalnaker, owner of Eastern Independent Torpedo Company, an expert in "well shooting", and a maverick in his own right. Packed in rubber-covered containers, 100 quarts of nitro-glycerine were carefully loaded into the Stinson, along with a dozen sticks of dynamite shoved under the seat.

Transferring nitro-glycerine from Stinson Detroiter to ground transport. Pilot Freddie McCall is facing camera and holding the volatile canister.

Strong headwinds on the trip home used up extra fuel, and by the time McCall reached Calgary, he literally landed on fumes. A crowd of more than 50 people had braved the cold weather to watch him come in to the airfield — either to cheer his return from an amazing expedition or to witness an explosion of unimaginable magnitude.

The Stinson bumped twice as it hit on the hard frozen ground of the airstrip and rolled to a stop quite a distance from the hangar, completely out of gas. A nervous ground crew came out to carefully refill the tank so McCall could taxi over the bumpy frozen ground to complete his journey to the front of the hangar.

When mechanic Earl Stinson (no relation to the manufacturer of the aircraft) started to unload the first crate of nitro-glycerine and began carting it away, McCall suddenly yelled out in alarm. He pointed to the lit cigarette hanging from Stinson's lips — that was too much risk even for the fearless McCall.

Maverick in the Sky

When interviewed about the volatile nature of the unique cargo, Charles Stalnaker minimized the danger of flying with what he called the "soup."

"Anything from broken axles and tire blowouts to collisions and bad bumps can happen to a truck on the road," he said to reporters. "It is very much safer in the air where only the pilot and shooter would be killed, whereas if it went off in a truck on the ground, many might be killed or injured."

That was only their first load. The next day, McCall and Stalnaker returned for a second shipment of 100 quarts of nitro — but this time they stopped in Lethbridge to refuel, to avoid another empty tank scenario. Upon delivery of the second load, the volatile cargo was carefully trucked to the oil well site at Turner Valley, and the charge exploded that night. McCall had saved the company many weeks of delay, plus the cost of expensive machinery and idle personnel.

RISKY BUSINESS

The adventures and misadventures both personal and professional did not stop as McCall continued in his role as Calgary's much loved son and leader in aviation matters.

Aviation was certainly a risky business, especially with more and more people taking to the skies for recreation as well as commercial purposes. McCall's Calgary Aero Club now led all Canadian flying clubs with its membership of 824. It was the largest organization of its kind on the North American continent, and the second largest in the world (after the club in Sydney, Australia). Thanks in part to McCall, pilots who were destined to become well known in Canadian aviation history, including Gil McLaren, Archie McMullen, Don Kepler, and Joe Patton, graduated with commercial licences from the flying school.

But "flying free" — like the pioneer aviators were used to — had become less acceptable. The aviation industry in general, and air shows and stunt flying in particular, had come to the attention of regulators, and the subjects of insurance and

Fly-in at new municipal airport in Renfrew district, Calgary, 1930. The Calgary Aero Club's two Cirrus Moths, seen above, took part.

airport fees likewise surfaced at city council meetings. Airway companies were informed they must indemnify the city against claims for damages, as a protection to resident householders in the case of an accident. The hefty amounts ($20,000 for any one accident, and $10,000 for property damage) sent the companies into shock. Fortunately, McCall became the arbitrator for this sticky situation, suggesting that the insurance companies be approached about a blanket policy on all airplanes operating from the airport to lower the premiums.

Increasing the safety of aviation included improving the lighting at airports. On November 21, 1929, McCall, followed by Jock Palmer in a second Great Western Airways aircraft, had the privilege of testing the new airport lights at Calgary. This innovation gave Calgary the distinction of having the first lighted airport in Canada, and thus the first Canadian airport that could receive night flights. The following summer, one of the most powerful aeronautical beacons in the world was installed 300 feet above ground level atop the Hudson's Bay store roof, to guide fliers to the city.

The third annual air show, sponsored by the Calgary Aero Club in 1930, was planned by a stellar organizing committee

Maverick in the Sky

Farther down the line, far right, is Emil Sick's Stinson Detroiter, with pilot Jock Palmer and mechanic Earl Stinson standing in front, and pilot Freddie McCall leaning on wing.

Freddie McCall piloting Calgary Aero Club's deHavilland Tiger Moth, circa 1934.

Daring Adventures

comprised of a Mr. Gee as president, with members T.L. Comba, W.L. Rutledge, Fred McCall, Joe Patton, Dr. Hesson, and F. Johnson. The show opened with sham dogfights with ex-wartime pilots, followed by dead-stick landings, aerial relay races, balloon busting competitions, a bombing competition of moving objects on the airport field, and exhibition stunt flying.

The *Herald* complimented the varied and thrilling, yet "sanely conducted," show. And even the stunt flying, always demanded by the public at such exhibitions, "was done within the proper bounds and without hazard to the onlookers."

Even with these adjustments and improvements, no one could prevent the Great Depression and its effect on the aviation industry. Like many companies and individuals, Great Western Airways went into receivership in January 1932, and its assets were dispersed. To pay the bills, McCall once again had to seek full-time work outside the aviation industry.

Meanwhile, Jim Lougheed, a member of the Calgary Aero Club who later became a World War II RCAF pilot, had purchased G-CANI. In 1934, during a test flight following a major overhaul, McCall was at the controls when the aircraft came into contact with a hill near Cochrane. The Stinson Detroiter that had made so many newsworthy trips at the hands of its famous captain was damaged beyond repair, although fortunately McCall walked away from the accident unscathed.

The Stinson Detroiter meets an untimely end.

Maverick in the Sky

CHAPTER 9

The Home Front

During the tough years of the Great Depression, the McCall family banded together. In 1933–34, three generations of McCalls lived together, with Freddie, Gen, and children Gerrie and Fred, as well as Freddie's sister Marjorie, her husband, Robert Scott, and young son, Jim all sharing in James and Agnes's two-storey house on 1st Street East.

Fortunately, Freddie and his dad got along well, since James was proud of his son for his war record and other achievements, even though he was not currently financially independent. For the children it was a wonderful plan that meant trips with Granddad, "Mr. Power", to the electrical plant. They'd watch the coal being dumped into great furnaces, and when James asked the men to open up the fire doors, they could see and hear the roaring flames. Young Fred remembers it was "like looking into Hell — really exciting stuff!" James would then take them to see the steam being produced that turned the generators to provide electricity.

Marjorie's husband, Robert Scott, also had a "powerful" job working for the railroad and moving engines around in the roundhouse, which the children loved to watch. The dozen or so big steam engines huffed and puffed and banged and crashed alarmingly. Freddie would often take his young son and nephew to the CPR roundhouse in the Alyth Yards, where Freddie's reputation as a Great War hero allowed him — and the children — privileges not usually offered. They would be allowed to climb aboard the engine cabs while they were being serviced and moved back and forth in the roundhouse. If the McCall grandchildren needed anything to convince them that they were part of a "powerful" family, these experiences clinched it.

In the midst of this time of financial concern, McCall received a recruiting letter from Edward "Eddie" Rickenbacker. At the time the famous U.S. World War I air ace was running Rickenbacker's Flying Circus, performing air stunts at fairs around the United States. Flying the World War I fighters such as Spads, Nieuports, and Sopwith Camels was admittedly a rather dangerous business, and although money was scarce, Gen refused to let Freddie go.

GROUNDED!

During this time, the seemingly invincible McCall met with personal misfortune — and it all came about innocently enough with a visit to the barber. Like Samson, his power dissolved with a haircut. McCall developed folliculitis, commonly known as "barber's itch", a normally minor ailment caused by damaged follicles that have become infected. While treating the condition, he accidentally got some ointment in his left eye, and the subsequent infection caused the loss of sight in this eye. Although it happened at a time when McCall wasn't flying, his son, Fred, remembers that it still came as a shock for his father to realize that he would have to give up his pilot's licence. His flying career sadly over, he had to relinquish his private licence, but kept the commercial licence as a keepsake.

From 1932 until 1940, McCall worked as a salesman for an oil development company, Calgary Brokers Ltd. It was a good job, and the family could again rent their own place. In those years, McCall would still make visits to the airport at Renfrew Field, and would take along his wife and son. The hangar was a half-round Quonset-shaped building, painted yellow. Jock Palmer, a fellow Great War flier who later became a well-known Southern Alberta commercial pilot, was building his own airplane there. The pungent smell of airplane dope overwhelmed them when they opened the door and went inside. "Jock, a big amiable guy, and Dad and his cronies would get together and they'd pitch pennies against the wall," Fred recalls. "The person who threw the penny closest to the wall won the pot. This was great sport." It was also a great excuse for Freddie to spend time at the airport, even if he couldn't fly.

Gen, meanwhile, would be sitting outside in the car, reading. Her main reason for coming at all was to keep track of her son, who seemed a little too eager to go flying with anybody who would take him up. She parked the car where she could clearly see the taxiway. If she saw young Fred getting into an airplane, she'd punch the horn and shake her finger, "No, no, no!"

The wings of the Cirrus and Gypsy Moths could be unpinned and pulled back to make more space in the hangar. When the men would push them outside and then button the wings up, Gen would be closely watching the airplanes to make sure Fred didn't climb in. Only later did she learn that he'd simply crawl inside an aircraft before it left the hangar, in the rear or front cockpit depending on the aircraft, and hunch down beneath the cowling so she couldn't see him as they taxied by. Of course, Freddie would turn his "blind eye" to such goings-on, undoubtedly proud of his aviation-loving son.

HOME SWEET HOME

Another family move followed in 1938, this time to the Elbow Park district. The McCalls would often rent a house until school finished in June, and then move out to Sylvan Lake and rent a cottage there for the summer. Freddie would come out on the weekends. Other relatives — aunts, uncles, and cousins — would generally come as well, to spend glorious carefree summers at the lake. When they returned to Calgary in the fall, Freddie and Gen would look for another house to rent. One year the family lived in the York Hotel for several weeks before they found suitable accommodations.

The social life of the McCalls finally came back in full swing. In 1939, Captain Freddie was doing quite well financially so the family moved to a furnished house on Premier Way, in Calgary's prestigious Mount Royal area. The house came with a billiard table in the basement, and McCall, a good player, taught his son, who soon excelled in the game. It became another source of pride for Freddie to see "the kid beat the old guys" at their game.

Working at a steady job, McCall was now able to spend more time with his family. They would go hunting together after school, and Fred remembers his father being a very good marksman, no doubt from his war experience. They'd bring home partridges and prairie chickens for dinner. Freddie would also have young Fred get on his goal pads and equipment and he'd shoot pucks at him for hours — "to sharpen my skills or break my legs, I wasn't sure which!" Fred jokes now.

Freddie McCall and young son Fred, age seven, proudly standing beside Freddie's first Packard car (circa 1935).

Older sister Gerrie was a maverick like her dad, which got her into trouble on occasion. One time, McCall saw his own Packard car being worked on at his friend's shop. Freddie went up to the young fellow who was having a dent repaired, and said, "Nice car you've got there. You had it a long time?" "Oh, not a long time," the boy replied, clearly uneasy. "Do you know, that's *my* car!" Freddie exclaimed in a gruff voice. The young man nearly dropped in his tracks. He and Gerrie had been out in the car and had bent a fender, but Gerrie was afraid to tell her father so she'd said, "Just get it fixed!"

McCall seemed to naturally stand out from the crowd and attract attention, even in his selection of a family dog. One day, during a visit to Banff, Freddie spotted a man walking two beautiful enormous dogs. He instantly fell in love with their appearance and demeanour. The man said that he bred these dogs from his kennel in Vancouver, and before the day was out Freddie had made a deposit on an order for one. Shortly thereafter, the young animal arrived by train after enduring a long and arduous trip chained up in a baggage car. The rail employees had been afraid to go near him because of his size. That is how the Great Dane, Rockmuk Romulus III, known as Rocky, became McCall's new best friend.

McCall took Rocky everywhere, enjoying the stares of passers-by at the handsome small-built man and large-built dog parading through Calgary's streets. One day he took the dog to the popular bar in the National Hotel in Inglewood, for an after-work brew. "You can't keep that dog in here, Mr. McCall!" announced the distressed bartender. McCall smiled and nodded toward Rocky. "You tell the dog," he answered. Rocky stayed to share the action and attention that always seemed to surround Capt. McCall.

WARTIME MEMORIES

Some war veterans choose to forget what they've seen and done in combat and never speak about it, while others' lives forever revolve around their feats, real or imagined. Freddie McCall fell into both camps.

"He was a funny guy," son Fred recalls. "When he was sober — which was most of the time — he was quiet, almost withdrawn, but put a couple of Scotches in him and he became very outgoing. Mom and Dad loved to party and had the kind of friends who did as well. They had a good time, and

I guess you could say they all revolved at the top of the social circle in Calgary in those days."

Freddie had a suitcase containing his memorabilia, which would often be brought out as the storytelling sessions got going. Out would come clippings from newspapers, magazine stories, a small piece of fabric off the Red Baron's airplane (which had been given to some fighter pilots active at the time of von Richthofen's death), letters from Fritz Blumenthal, Freddie's medals, citations, and his cap and wings, and the stories that went along with them.

Gen would sit patiently, listening to the action stories and recollections of old friends, so many of whom hadn't made it home. She shared stories of her own as well, from her years working with the Red Cross in Calgary during the war, and during the devastating flu epidemic of 1918. In fact, Gen's stories often matched Freddie's for drama and poignancy.

In preparation for regular post-war mess dinners with his ex-military pals, Freddie would don his dress blues, and ask his son to polish the brass buttons, his medals, and his boots. Looking ready for inspection when he left, he'd come home looking slightly different.

At one mess dinner in 1938, the boys got bragging about who might be the bravest of them all. To outdo the others, Freddie declared that he could pet Carmichael, a very famous polar bear at the Calgary Zoo. "Oh no, you can't," was the goading response. To settle the debate, a group headed off to the zoo right after the dinner. True to his wager, McCall reached through the bars and petted Carmichael on the head. No problem. That was pretty tame.

Then he upped the ante. "I can pet the damned lion, too."

"Oh no, you can't!"

Ever-courageous Freddie reached into the cage to stroke the big lion named Leo. But the lion didn't like being petted by the man, famous pilot or not, and promptly bit off the middle finger of his right hand, right down past the first knuckle.

Capt. McCall (in uniform, close to camera) at a mess dinner in 1938, just hours before his encounter with the lion. Note that all fingers on his left hand are still intact!

Freddie's friends wheeled him over to the Calgary General Hospital.

Son Fred remembers his dad coming home that night, looking very sober and sheepish, with a large bandage on his finger. "Mother was not pleased."

CHAPTER 10

Recall to Duty

"FREDDIE'S BACK IN HARNESS AGAIN!" WAS THE INSPIRING NEWS BROADCAST IN AVIATION CIRCLES, BOTH AT HOME AND ABROAD, WHEN ON SEPTEMBER 19, 1940, ONE YEAR AFTER WORLD WAR II WAS DECLARED, McCALL ANSWERED A REQUEST FOR HIS SERVICES.

At the outbreak of the war, a unique action program called the British Commonwealth Air Training Plan (BCATP) had been quickly put into place by Canada, the United Kingdom, Australia, and New Zealand. Canada was charged with setting up schools across the country and fast-forwarding the training of air and ground crews. With aviation slated to play an even bigger role in this war than in its predecessor, there was a desperate need for pilots, navigators, bomb aimers, wireless operators, air gunners, and flight engineers.

The BCATP officials scoured the land, from the bush to the boardroom, appealing to regional flying clubs, commercial aviation companies, Department of Transport offices, and military veterans for personnel to share their expertise. Experienced, knowledgeable aviators such as Captain McCall, DSO, MC & Bar, DFC received letters from Ottawa, beseeching them to come back into service — as role models and teachers. McCall gave up a successful career in the oil business to again serve his country.

Canada's own air force had been formed in 1924, but while Canadians could now wear their distinct Royal Canadian Air Force (RCAF) shoulder badges, for active overseas service they would be assigned to national squadrons within the Royal Air Force and trained under the RAF policies. Former RAF captain McCall thus went to Toronto — now with

Maverick in the Sky

Squadron Leader McCall again answered the call to serve
his country, in World War II.

the equivalent rank in the RCAF of flight lieutenant — as a
ground instructor.

When the *Calgary Herald* published an article on McCall's
return to service, one of his old World War I flying-mates
overseas happened to read it. Lieut. B.S.B. Andrews was delighted to find that his wartime pal was still alive and well. He
had long thought that McCall had died from influenza after
being sent home to Canada from the Front. "I was an observer

in the 13th Squadron and had the pleasure and honour of flying with Freddie and being in more than one show for which he was decorated," Andrews wrote to the newspaper. "You can take it from me that what you say about him was no exaggeration, as he was a great pilot, and Heaven help 'Jerry' if his pupils turn out as good as Freddie was." He planned to pass the word in England because it would surely help morale.

One day Flt. Lieut. McCall was on parade in Toronto. His unit was being inspected by Air Vice-Marshal K.M. Guthrie, a renowned fighter pilot in World War I who had stayed with the RCAF after the war. As Guthrie was moving down the line, he spotted Freddie standing in front of his troops. He broke away from the entourage and rushed over to shake his hand. "Freddie McCall!" he exclaimed. "How the hell are you?" Such a greeting in the midst of a very formal inspection completely broke protocol and startled the senior officers managing the parade.

On January 1, 1942, McCall was promoted to squadron leader. Temporary duty assignments such as disciplinary hearings took him to various locations across Canada. When McCall was sent to Saskatoon as Commanding Officer of the Initial Training School, in addition to his military duties he was often invited to perform as a public speaker. His reputation, energy, and charisma served to raise funds for the war effort and also to boost morale.

One evening he was asked to speak to Rotary Club members. He started by expressing his amazement at how well trained the pilots of this war were, compared to his experiences in World War I. "Aviation today is a science," he told his audience. "When I transferred from the infantry to the Royal Flying Corps, I was given 1 hour and 40 minutes' solo flying, and sent out to fight. The aircraft had a top speed of 45 miles an hour, and sometimes we flew at an altitude of 500 feet. Now, students in the air force have an eight-week course at an Initial Training School where it is decided whether they are best suited to be pilots or something else." McCall was clearly thrilled to be a part of this new era, and to play a role in preparing young men to serve their country.

ON THE HOME FRONT

While McCall was back in the service and travelling all over the country, the rest of his family remained at the Athlone Apartments on 19th Avenue West, where for the first time they'd needed to buy furniture. They tried to do their part for the war effort, too. At times, there would be as many as five or six extra young men crowded around the table in the small apartment, military recruits stationed at the Calgary-based BCATP training schools who had come from all over the Commonwealth. Weekend dinner invitations to the McCall home were highly prized, not only to help relieve barracks-boredom, but also to enjoy Gen's fine cooking and Gerrie's and Fred's friendliness, and to bask in the aura of Freddie's fame.

Freddie often had a weekend pass to fly home as a passenger on training aircraft. Arriving to see a roomful of young uniformed recruits, he liked to stop midway through the door and say in a loud officer's voice, "Who the hell are you?" The young pilot officers would stare in shock and jump to attention when they saw Squadron Leader McCall with his chest emblazoned with medals. Here was a man who'd shot down 37 enemy airplanes and had lived to come back and tell the tale! "Sorry, sir!" they'd cry in unison, their faces red and eyes respectfully downcast. Then McCall would laugh, put them at ease, and welcome them to his home.

Some of the recruits came to visit more than once, and Gerrie soon found herself engaged to one of them, a young British pilot named Andy Brown. Andy became a bomber pilot, multi-engine, and in 1943 was sent to fly over The Hump in Burma. There he disappeared, never to be found. Because he had listed Gerrie as his next of kin, the telegram came to the McCall house. It was a pretty bad day, Fred recalled.

Gerrie eventually moved into her own apartment, but in

the same building as her family, just down the hall from her parents and younger brother, who was still in school. Around this time she became interested in the family's genealogy. She found out more than she bargained for when a firm in Scotland that traced family history and heraldry (the Lyon Office and Standing Council of Scottish Chiefs) told her that the name McCall actually stemmed from McColl. When the laird of the McColl family died, the family estate was passed on to the eldest son, as was the custom in the day. In protest, the younger son had broken away and taken a band of faithful serfs with him. Changing the spelling of the McColl name to McCall, he then made his living by stealing sheep from the older brother's estate!

DANGER IS SWEET

The ancient history of the McCalls may have been clouded, with ties claimed to both the MacDonald and MacAulay clans, but the family was amused by the story. They were more impressed by the clan motto that seemed to better suit the McColl/McCall descendants: *Dulce Periculum* — Danger Is Sweet.

Indeed, Freddie's son was already following in his father's danger-seeking footsteps. In 1940, at age 12, Fred had joined the army cadets, like his father before him. (There was still no air cadet unit in Calgary at that time.) A keen rifle shot taught by his father, Fred collected rifles and enjoyed practising his shooting.

One day, however, when Fred was only 16, his adventures with guns took a dangerous turn. He and his friends liked to hike and camp west of Calgary in the Sarcee area, where one corner of the reserve lands had been taken over by the military for training and artillery ranges. The cadets took their rifles onto the streetcar up 17th Avenue to the end of the line, and then walked out to Sarcee to hunt gophers.

On the morning of December 7, 1945 — four years to the day following Pearl Harbor's bombing — Fred stumbled onto a two-inch mortar shell. "It was lying right there on the ground, so we kicked it around. That wasn't too clever. We thought it was a dud but it wasn't and it went off." Two of the boys were hit and Fred was seriously wounded. Fortunately, the doctor who saw him had just returned from overseas, and was very experienced with shrapnel wounds.

The incident occasioned a military board of inquiry, with two officers conducting an investigation into the leftover live shell. For some unknown reason, when they came to interview Fred's parents, they were carrying pistols. Freddie, still in military service, was not too impressed with these guys. According to Fred, "I guess they were acting kind of officious, but when they sat down, one guy's pistol fell out onto the floor. Pretty embarrassing. Father just about threw him out of the house. The end result was the acknowledgement that it was an accident, and that was all there was to it."

CARRYING THE TORCH

Young Fred went on to become the fifth person in Canada to achieve the level of master cadet, and received his commission with the Cadet Services of Canada. He was also a corporal in the King's Own Calgary Regiment (Calgary Tanks) where he was further coached by another expert marksman.

But when a commanding officer of a light anti-aircraft unit found out what his friend Freddie's kid was doing, he told him to come and see him. Because he already had a commission, Fred was invited to join the unit. It has to be said that he lied about his age, and was just 16 years old when he became a second lieutenant in the 68th Light Anti-Aircraft Regiment with the Canadian Militia, beginning an illustrious military career for a second generation of McCalls.

During the time Fred was serving with the Royal Canadian Horse Artillery, he ended up logging a good deal of backseat flying with the regiment's Air OP Flight (Air Observation Post). If he'd had the choice, he would have preferred to be in the front seat, like his father. Fred ended up with 27 years' active service, and received his own medals, the Order of Military Merit (OMM) and Canadian Forces Decoration (CD). Both Freddie and Gen were naturally pleased with their son's career choice, carrying on, as he was, the McCall family honour and heritage of military service.

Meanwhile, for the remainder of World War II, Freddie served as an administrator, commanding an Initial Training School in Saskatoon. The BCATP was enormously successful — the most massive and effective single aviation training program in history. At its height, it involved students from the United Kingdom, Australia, New Zealand, South Africa, Southern Rhodesia, and Canada, with over half the 131,553 grads being Canadian.

At last, with Canadians making these and other important contributions, an end to the war was in sight. On D-Day, June 6, 1944, the Allied forces had landed on France's Normandy coast, to begin the liberation of Western Europe. The fighting went on for almost another year, however, until May 8, 1945, V-E (Victory in Europe) Day, which marked the final surrender of German forces. With Canadian, U.S., and British forces advancing from the west, Soviet forces closing in from the east, and Adolf Hitler dead, Grand Admiral Doenitz formally signed the surrender to end the war in Europe. Japan finally surrendered on August 14, 1945, V-J (Victory in Japan) Day, and World War II came to an end with an Allied victory — after six years of conflict and the sacrifice of more than 45,000 Canadian lives.

A month later, on September 11, 1945, McCall was able to retire again from the air force, this time from the RCAF as a squadron leader. He was awarded further medals for his incredible collection — the Canadian Volunteer Service Medal (CVSM), and a Victory Medal.

And so Freddie McCall, at 49 years of age, with greying hair and missing a right middle finger from his encounter not with war but with a lion, returned to Calgary and to the oil business.

Last Post. Close-out Flight Plan. Freddie McCall is laid to rest in the Field of Honour, Calgary's Burnsland Cemetery, January 1949.

TERMINATION OF THE FLIGHT PLAN

A few years later, Freddie and Gen were on their way to Lloydminster when their car slipped on the wintry roads and hit the ditch. They suffered bruises and a few minor cuts. A short time afterwards, on January 22, 1949, they were at home in the Athlone Apartments listening to the Macdonald Brier curling bonspiel radio broadcast. Freddie was lying on the couch when Gen heard him say, "Oh, Gen!" She came into the room, and saw that he was gone. He'd suffered a blood clot, perhaps as a result of that unfortunate car accident, and it was all over peacefully for the famous flier. He was dead at the early age of 53 years.

The funeral was held that week at Grace Presbyterian Church in Calgary. "Freddie McCall's search for life left him hurtling through the skies seeking adventure. Indeed, he earned the title of a father of aviation in the West, and a pioneer of commercial flying in Western Canada. In the interpretation of Heaven, all angels have wings," Reverend Dr. Frank Morley intoned, "and so Heaven could be thought of as a place for flying."

The service was followed by a graveside ceremony, at which "Reveille" and "The Last Post" sounded. Squadron Leader McCall's RCAF officer's cap rested atop the flag-draped casket. In attendance were 55 officers and men of Calgary's three air force stations, including VIPs such as Air Vice-Marshal K.M. Guthrie, alongside aviation colleagues and citizens who'd long admired Freddie's antics and efforts. Lieut. Fred McCall, in uniform, saluted as the Honour Guard fired their volleys over his father's grave. Freddie's grieving wife Gen, daughter Gerrie, and future-daughter-in-law Dixie stood at the foot of the coffin. Large soft snowflakes rested lightly on the bowed heads and shoulders of the many mourners who had come to say farewell to one of Canada's greatest aviators. He was laid to rest, most appropriately, in the Field of Honour in Calgary's Burnsland Cemetery.

EPILOGUE:
Afterlife of
a Canadian Hero

Few men are born with such amazing ability, and luck, to fly a cloth-covered biplane into the heart of aerial warfare and come out the victor — in more than 100 missions in a mere eight months. Through his subsequent and equal determination to do everything possible to build Calgary's civil aviation scene through his barnstorming, establishing the Calgary Aero Club, running aviation companies on a shoestring, making medical evacuations, and pioneering new routes, Freddie McCall would not be forgotten.

McCall Field

Just seven years after McCall's untimely death, a state-of-the-art airport terminal was completed in his home town. The Calgary Aviation Commission decided it was the perfect time to acquaint newcomers with the city's past by renaming the airport in McCall's honour. Although not everyone on city council agreed with the motion, Arthur R. Smith, MLA, a former alderman, was insistent that the name of Calgary's airport should be the proper memorial for the great pilot. The *Calgary Herald* also supported the idea: "It was men such as McCall who wrote Canada's name in the early flying history, and then he returned home to Calgary to devote his life to the development of flying when it was truly a wing and a prayer business. Was the daring pilot who had served in two wars, and worked so valiantly to put Calgary on the aviation map, already forgotten, just seven years after his death?" McCall, who never backed down from a good scrap, might have en-

Gen McCall and son Fred view the plaque renaming Calgary's airfield "McCall Field."

joyed the debate. The airport was finally named "Calgary Municipal Airport — McCall Field."

On Remembrance Day, Sunday, November 11, 1956, the plaque was unveiled. Lieut. Fred R. McCall, Royal Canadian Artillery (RCA), Winnipeg, wore his father's many medals pinned to the right side of his tunic, and three generations of McCalls joined representatives from the city, the armed forces, the Royal Canadian Legion, and Air Cadets. Also in the gathering was another famous Calgary pilot, McCall's old friend Jock Palmer.

Freddie would have been delighted to know that, by 1958, McCall Field boasted two major runways to handle the largest jets, plus two smaller runways used as taxi strips for light aircraft. A fine new terminal building, advertised as "the most modern in Canada," had opened and the field also accommodated a number of large hangars. Aviation services sprang up because Calgary now had more locally based private aircraft than any other Canadian city. As Calgary's airport gained international status and became known as Calgary International Airport, the McCall Field appellation remained, and is still used by those who remember the man, and what he means to aviation history.

Nearby, and within the provincial electoral district designated Calgary-McCall, a short roadway leading from McKnight Boulevard toward the south end of airport lands was named McCall Way. Fittingly, the Aero Space Museum of Calgary is situated at this address and nearby lies the McCall Lake Golf Course.

CITIZEN OF THE CENTURY

The honours bestowed on McCall continued well after his passing. Squadron Leader McCall was inducted into Canada's Aviation Hall of Fame on July 7, 1978, joining old friends like Wop May, Punch Dickins, Don MacLaren, and Jock Palmer. The induction citation read: "His exquisite mastery of primitive military aeronautics, and his dedication to opening new routes of air travel through mountainous areas, have been of outstanding benefit to Canadian aviation."

When Calgary celebrated its centenary in 1994, Freddie McCall was the People's Choice for Calgary's outstanding citizen of the century for his contribution to aviation. In 1999, when the Royal Canadian Air Force, Canadian Forces Air Command, celebrated its 75th anniversary, McCall was the featured poster boy. In a ceremony held at Calgary's Aero Space Museum in 2001, Captain McCall was posthumously awarded the Neil J. Armstrong Memorial Award for his extraordinary aviation accomplishments.

In 2003, at a "Calgarians of the Clouds" formal mess dinner of the Honourable Guard and Special Friends of the Museum of the Regiments, McCall was recognized, along with compatriot World War II hero William McKnight, DFC & Bar. While McCall had returned from active service,

McKnight, unfortunately, had not. That evening, McCall's son, Fred Robert McCall, OMM, CD, was awarded the rank of Senior Honorary Commander in the Honourable Guard in recognition of his own services to Canada and its aviation heritage. His father would have been proud.

MENTOR AND MAVERICK

The Calgary Aero Club, McCall's pride and joy, is still training pilots under the name of the Calgary Flying Club. During World War II, when the BCATP was active, the club had operated No. 5 Elementary Training School, first in Lethbridge and later in High River. Following cessation of the war, the club had returned to Calgary as a civilian school. Now located west of Calgary at Springbank Airport, the Calgary Flying Club still honours Captain McCall as its mentor and first president.

In 2007, the Glenbow Museum of Calgary opened a long-term "Mavericks of Alberta" exhibit. Featured in the War and the Home Front display is the story of Squadron Leader [confirm with Fred] McCall, DSO, MC & Bar, DFC. Also featured is a full-scale replica, devotedly built by Fred McCall and crew, of the Curtiss JN-4 that his father so famously stalled on top of the merry-go-round in 1919. "If he were here now, he would be pretty pleased," Fred McCall said to a *Calgary Herald* reporter.

McCall's adventurous spirit might have been inherited from the clan motto, *Dulce Periculum*. It certainly defined the manner in which he had lived his life. McCall's amazing wartime accomplishments, his extraordinary flying skills, his fiercely independent, adventuresome, "barnstorming" character, and his self-reliant, entrepreneurial spirit, make him eminently eligible to be remembered and honoured as one of Alberta's revered mavericks.

Captain Freddie McCall in front of his Curtiss Jenny, July 1919.

Son, Major Fred McCall, in front of his Curtiss Jenny, June 2007.
This full-scale replica aircraft is featured in the "Mavericks of
Alberta" exhibit, Glenbow Museum, Calgary.

Epilogue: Afterlife of a Canadian Hero

Appendices

McCALL'S WORLD WAR I RECORD

NOTE: According to log books and other sources: some lists show 37 victories, some 35, and some up to 44. Gaps in British records, as well as "half-point" shared victories, tend to confuse official counts; for example, some records fail to note the two further victories on April 15th and 16th. All dates are in 1918.

No.	Date	Type of A/C	Place	Result
1	Jan 6	Albatros DV Scout	Estaires	Crashed
2	Mar 6	Albatros DV Scout	Estaires	Crashed
3	Mar 27	Rumpler C 2-seater	Estaires	Crashed
4	Apr 15	Albatros DV Scout	Beaucamps	Out of control
5	Apr 16	DFW	Bray	Out of control
6	May 25	DFW	Estaires	Out of control
7	May 29	DFW	Estaires	Shot down in flames
8	May 30	DFW	Beaucamps	Out of control
9	Jun 9	DFW	Mézières	Crashed
10	Jun 12	Albatros DV Scout	Lieneres	Driven down
11	Jun 12	DFW	La Motte	Driven down
12	Jun 13	DFW	Montdidier	Crashed
13	Jun 16	Fokker DVII	Combles	Crashed
14	Jun 27	Halberstadt	Goyencourt	Crashed
15	Jun 27	Pfalz DIII	Bray	Out of control
16	Jun 28	Rumpler C 2-seater	Belloy	Crashed
17	Jun 28	Halberstadt	Bray	Crashed
18	Jun 28	Pfalz DIII	Bray	Out of control
19	Jun 28	Albatros DV Scout	Bray	Out of control
20	Jun 30	Albatros DV Scout	Bray	Shot down in flames
21	Jun 30	Albatros DV Scout	Cappy	Crashed

No.	Date	Type of A/C	Place	Result
22	Jun 30	Albatros DV Scout	Caix	Crashed
23	Jun 30	Fokker DVII	Warsy	Out of control
24	Jun 30	Albatros DV Scout	Albert	Out of control
25	Jul 1	Albatros DV Scout	La Motte	Out of control
26	Jul 3	Fokker DVII	Bayonvillers	Shot down in flames
27	Jul 3	Fokker DVII	Bayonvillers	Out of control
28	Jul 4	Fokker DVII	Proyart	Out of control
29	Jul 7	Albatros C 2-seater	La Boissiere	Out of control
30	Jul 30	Albatros C 2-seater	Guillaucourt	Crashed
31	Jul 31	Albatros C 2-seater	Pozieres	Crashed
32	Aug 1	Albatros C 2-seater	Cantalmaison	Crashed
	Aug 4	Two balloons	Caix	Crashed
33	Aug 9	Fokker DVII	Bray	Shot down in flames
34	Aug 9	Fokker DVII	Carnoy	Crashed
35	Aug 11	Fokker DVII	Estrées	Crashed
36	Aug 12	Fokker DVII	Estrées	Forced landing
37	Aug 12	Fokker DVII	Guillaucourt	Crashed

Maverick in the Sky

THE 10 TOP-SCORING CANADIAN FIGHTER PILOTS OF THE BRITISH EMPIRE IN WORLD WAR I

- Major William A. Bishop (72),
  with Squadrons 21, 60 and 86

- Major Raymond Collishaw (62),
  with Squadrons 3 (N), 10 (N), 13 (N), 203 and 47

- Captain Donald M. MacLaren (54)
  with Squadron 46

- Major William G. Barker (52),
  with Squadrons 9, 4, 15, 28, 66, 139 and 201

- Captain Fred Robert McCall (37),
  with Squadrons 13 and 41

- Captain William G. Claxton (36),
  with Squadron 41

- Captain J. Stuart T. Fall (34),
  with Squadrons 3 (N), 4 (N), and 9 (N)

- Captain Alfred C. Atkey (33), with Squadrons 18 and 22

- Major Albert D. Carter (31), with Squadron 19

- Captain Andrew E. McKeever (30), with Squadron 11

McCall's Roster of Postings in World War II:

- #7 ITS Saskatoon (July 15/42) *
- No. 2 Training Command, Winnipeg (Sept./42 — [date obscure])
- #6 Elementary Flying Training School, Prince Albert (April/43)
- #7 ITS, Saskatoon (June/44)
- #4 SFTS Saskatoon (July/44)
- Temporary Duty assignments to Fort St. John and Dawson Creek, B.C., and Whitehorse, YT, in 1944/45
- Edmonton (Oct./45)

* McCall, as so often happened, was given the most senior roles:
  - Honorary President, Sergeant's Mess,
  - President, Fire Committee,
  - President, Audit Board, WPF,
  - President, Station Funds Committee,
  - Honorary President, Grounds Committee, and
  - Honorary President, Band.

During his tenure with the BCATP, Squadron Leader Mc-Call commanded both the #7 ITS at Saskatoon and the Administrative Unit, North West Air Command, in Edmonton.

AUTHOR'S NOTE

Although Canada adopted metric measurements in 1971, the aviation industry continues to use Imperial measurements with regard to altitude (feet above sea level), speed (nautical or statute miles per hour), weight (pounds), fuel (measured by either weight in pounds or volume in gallons). During World War I, the U.K., the United States, and Canada used the Imperial system, while Germany employed the metric system. Even today, most aircraft instrument panels, especially those manufactured in the United States, display Imperial measurements. The author has elected to use Imperial measurements to ensure integrity and accuracy, and to minimize the clutter of conversion.

Acknowledgements

This book is dedicated to Fred and Dixie McCall, who encouraged and assisted me through their knowledge and complete store of anecdotes and artifacts regarding Fred's father, the famous Squadron Leader Freddie McCall, DSO, MC & Bar, DFC.

And it is dedicated to Michale Lang, then Vice President, Access, Collections & Exhibits, Glenbow Museum, Calgary. Michale got the ball rolling by contracting me as the researcher on Capt. McCall for the Glenbow's "Mavericks of Alberta" exhibit, and then said, "Why don't you write a book about Freddie?"

Thanks to these wonderful people, and many others, who assisted in so many ways.

In this book, I have quoted from personal interviews with Fred and Dixie McCall, conducted on January 14, February 13, 19, 27; March 3 in 2005, and many various dates throughout 2006 and 2007; the Record of Service of Temporary Captain Fred Robert McCall, DSO, DFC, MC; Royal Air Force Officers' Records, Ministry of Defence; and the article by Capt. McCall in *Aviation Annual 1921*, "Air Fighting in the World War — How it Developed from Slow Clumsy Machines to Demons of Speed". Two verses are taken from the 10-verse poem by Edna Jaques in the *Calgary Daily Herald* on Saturday, July 5, 1919, and further mentioned in *The Albertan* on November 1, 1972. Mrs. Jaques had written to the *Herald* asking where she might obtain a photo of herself sitting on the wing of McCall's airplane, which had been taken at the time of that flight in July of 1919 at Bowness Field.

Maverick in the Sky

Recommended Reading and Bibliography

Drew, Lieut. Col. George A. *Canada's Fighting Airmen*. The MacLean Publishing Company, Limited, Toronto, 1930, chapter on McCall

Ellis, Frank. *Canada's Flying Heritage*. University of Toronto Press, Toronto, 1954

Gowans, Bruce W. *Wings Over Calgary 1906–1940*. Historical Society of Alberta, Chinook Country Chapter, Calgary, 1990

Long Lance, C. de G., Capt. S.C. (ed.) *Aviation Annual, 1921* "Devoted to Flying in Alberta and the Furtherance of the Science of Aeronautics in Canada"; Forward by Brig.Gen. H.F. McDonald, CMG, DSO, MEIC: Calgary Aero Club (Capt. F.R. McCall, DSO, MC& Bar, DFC, Business Manager), Calgary, 1921

Murray, W. Roland. "Canada's Fifth Air Ace of the 1914–1918 War — Captain Fred. R. McCall, DSO, MC & Bar, DFC" (unpublished manuscript, 1969)

Robertson, Bruce (ed). *Air Aces of the 1914–1918 War*. Harleyford Publications Limited, Letchworth, Herts, UK, 1959

Shores, Christopher. *Air Aces*. Bison Books Corp, Greenwich, CT, USA, 1983

Shores, Christopher, Norman Franks, and Russell Guest. *Above the Trenches: A Complete Record of the Fighter Aces and Units of the British Empire Air Forces 1915-1920.* Fortress Publications Inc., Stoney Creek, Ontario, 1990

Wise, S.F. *Canadian Airmen and the First World War: The Official History of the Royal Canadian Air Force,* Vol. 1, Part Four: *Airpower in the Land Battle*, University of Toronto Press, 1980

Index

Maverick in the Sky

About the Author

Shirlee Smith Matheson is the author of numerous books on Canadian aviation, including Volumes I, II, and III of *Flying the Frontiers*; *Lost: True Stories of Canadian Aviation Tragedies*; and *A Western Welcome to the World -- The History of Calgary International Airport*. She is a charter member of Canadian Women in Aviation International (Alberta Rocky Mountain High chapter), and in 1999 was awarded The 99's Canadian Award in Aviation. She has also written two books on non-aviation subjects (*This Was Our Valley* and *Youngblood of the Peace*), has published six adventure novels for young people, and has written short stories and stage plays.

Shirlee has lived in all four Western Canadian provinces. For many years, she resided in the Peace River country of northeastern B.C., but now makes her home in Calgary, where she is employed at the Aero Space Museum. Check the author's website www.ssmatheson.ca for information on past and future publications.